Derrida and Indian Philosophy

Derrida and Indian Philosophy

Harold Coward

STATE UNIVERSITY OF NEW YORK PRESS

Published by
State University of New York Press, Albany

Printed in the United States of America

For information, address State University of New York Press, State University Plaza, Albany, N.Y., 12246

Library of Congress Cataloging-in-Publication Data

Coward, Harold G.
Derrida and Indian Philosophy / Harold Coward.
p. cm.
Includes bibliographical references.
ISBN 0–7914–0499–4 (alk. paper).
—ISBN 0–7914–0500–1 (pbk.: alk. paper)
1. Derrida, Jacques. 2. Philosophy, Indic. I. Title.
B2430.D484068 1990
194—dc20 90–32875
CIP

10 9 8 7 6 5 4 3

Contents

To my father,
Lincoln,
who has lived his life
in service to others

Acknowledgments

One of the many joys of working in an interdisciplinary research institute is that one's research interests are constantly stimulated from new and surprising directions. My interest in Derrida was seeded and developed by contact with literature scholars who have worked in the institute in the past few years. One particular event that focused my attention in this direction was a project that brought together writers of poetry and fiction, literary critics, and scholars of sacred scriptures to examine the way in which words do or do not evoke the transcendent. My coorganizer in this project was E. D. Blodgett, a poet and scholar of comparative literature. This book project has now been published as *Silence, The Word and the Sacred,* edited by E. D. Blodgett and H. G. Coward (Waterloo, Ontario: Wilfrid Laurier University Press, 1989). It was while sitting with Ted in the evening after a day of cross-country skiing in the Rockies, that our talk would turn to questions of the philosophy of language. These discussions with Ted produced the initial insights that formed a bridge between my own specialization in classical Indian philosophy of language and the thought of Jacques Derrida. Ted Blodgett not only got me started on this project, he read several chapters in early draft and I benefited much from his critique.

I was also fortunate in having Toby Foshay as an institute research fellow. Toby is not only knowledgeable about Derrida, he also knows Buddhism. His critique of my early attempts at relating Derrida to Indian philosophy were most valuable. The chapter on Derrida and Śaṅkara was first presented at a conference at Madras University, and there I received helpful comments from John Koller and Arthur Herman. In the case of the chapter on Nāgārjuna, a very sensitive critique offered by David Loy helped to enlarge my own approach, which had been strongly shaped by my teacher Professor T. R. V. Murti. Toby Foshay and David Loy will be joining me along with Mark Taylor, Morny Joy, and Michel Despland in another institute project—a continuation of our mutual interest in Derrida in the form of a book *Derrida and Negative Theology* to be published by SUNY Press in 1992.

A Killam Resident Research Fellowship in 1989 enabled me to complete the writing of this book. Thanks are due to Gerry Dyer and Cindy Atkinson for their careful typing of the manuscript. As always Bill Eastman and his staff at SUNY Press have made the careful work of publishing a pleasure.

January 6, 1990

Harold Coward
Professor of Religious Studies
and Director
Calgary Institute for the Humanities
University of Calgary

Introduction

VERY early in life, as early as I can remember, my mother told me Bible stories. These oral words had a deep and transforming effect upon my consciousness. For me as a young child the experience of hearing the word of Scripture provided the basis of my religious experience, and they remain the fundamental grounding of my life to this day. Later in church school, university, and seminary I studied the scriptural word as a written text. I learned to approach the Bible as literature, to examine its historical context, its literary sources, its structural forms, its canonization and interpretation. All of this naturally led on to a study of theology, philosophy, and psychology—always with language as the point of focus.

How is it that we experience the word? Although intellectually stimulating and enlightening, this analysis of the Bible and the philosophical and psychological function of language sometimes led to a dimming of the transforming power of God's word in my life. When I began to study Indian religion and philosophy, and its experience of Hindu scripture in particular, I became resensitized to the spiritual power of the Christian Scripture. The Hindu emphasis on the Veda as oral, and its downplaying of the written text made me think back to my early experience of hearing the parables of Jesus at my mother's knee. For the Hindu, the spoken sacred word reveals divine truth and has power to transform one's consciousness. In Indian thought writing is often devalued and seen only as a teaching or academic study aid. The end goal, however, aimed at actualizing the oral experience of language. Pāṇini's Sanskrit grammar, for example, is based on the oral experience of language and was taught and passed on from teacher to student in techniques of learning and memory that were fully oral in nature. All of this is developed into a full blown philosophy of language by Patañjali and Bhartṛhari.[1]

This study of Hindu scripture with its emphasis on the oral experience of the word and the philosophy of language it engendered led me to reflect on our modern Western way of thinking. Today most of us in the West simply take for granted that *scripture* means "holy writ," "holy writing, or "sacred book." Our focus both as lay people and religious studies scholars is on the written or printed character of a holy text. Little attention is given to its function as spoken and heard sacred word. This is also true for modern Western philosophy. Whereas Rhetoric once played a major role in Western philosophy, it has now fallen into disrepute in favor of analysis of written texts. The reasons for this emphasis upon the written rather than the oral word are not hard to find. In the recent past, at least, the West has emphasized the study and importance of the written text for both scholarly and devotional purposes.[2] Indeed the very words *scripture* (from the Latin *scriptura,* "a writing") and *bible* (from the Latin *biblia,* "a collection of writings" or "book") have led us to think of divine revelation as a written or printed object. This conception of scripture as written word is bolstered in our culture by the great importance that we attach to the written or printed word. Indeed one modern scholar has gone so far as to term writing the *humiliation of the word*[3]—a characterization that, as Derrida makes clear, is far too one-sided. Yet it is true that in many areas of life today we say that unless you have something in writing, it is not to be trusted. This valuation of the written over the oral-aural experience of language, although characteristic of the most recent period of Western cultural history, is, as Derrida shows us, part of a polarization that has been present in Western thought from the time of the Greeks.[4]

These reflections led me to examine the respective roles played by oral and written language in the major world religions. The results of my study demonstrated that whereas in all cases religious traditions began with the experience of an oral (and usually poetic) word, written language also played an important function in the preservation and intellectual study of the text. By the end of the book, however, I found myself privileging the oral over the written to the point of concluding that of the two it is the oral word in its relational context that has the greater power to transform lives.[5] I became aware that I was polarized in favor of the oral over against the written. This sense of intellectual imbalance led me, immediately, to a reading of Jacques Derrida. Here, I thought, I might find a balancing corrective—or at least a serious challenge—for Derrida constantly speaks of the importance of "writing." What I found in Derrida, however, was something much deeper. Derrida does of course effectively challenge any privileging of the oral over the written—the error that he thinks Western philosophy and theology have fallen into. But to see him as arguing for "writing" (and this is exactly the way John Searle and other analytic philosophers typically respond to Derrida[6]) is to misread Derrida and miss the depth of his position. Recognizing Derrida's rereading of the whole oral-written debate as shifting the analysis to a deeper level in an attempt to find a "middle way" I began to see many resonances to Indian philosophy—to the Buddhist critique of Nāgārjuna first, and later to Bhartṛhari's Hindu philosophy of language. In this way I came to write *Derrida and Indian Philosophy.* But before beginning our comparison of Derrida and Indian philosophy, let us briefly examine the traditional nature of Indian philosophy and its recent attempts to relate itself to Western philosophy.

TRADITIONAL INDIAN PHILOSOPHY

In a book that seeks to relate Derrida to Indian philosophy some introductory explanations might prove helpful to those unfamiliar with Indian thought. Different conceptions of philosophy prevailed in India at different times. In his review of philosophy in India, K. Satchidananda Murty mentions three specific conceptions.[7] First, there is the view that philosophy is the rational, critical, and illuminating review of the contents of theology, economics, and political science. This view is technically termed *Ānvikṣiki* and is seen as establishing the foundation of all action and duty. Second, philosophy is seen as a system of ideas comprising epistemology, metaphysics, ethics, and soteriology. The technical Sanskrit name for systems of that sort is *Darśana.* The third approach in India views philosophy as an intuitive network of views regarding humanity, its nature and destiny, Nature, and the Ultimate Reality or God, explicit or implicit in the sayings, songs, hymns, talks, and writings of mystics, sages, and saints; this form may be called *popular philosophy.* In relating Indian philosophy to Western thought, and especially to the philosophy of Jacques Derrida, the first two conceptions—philosophy as *Ānvikṣiki* or the foundation of all action and philosophy as *Darśana* or metaphysics and soteriology—are engaged.

The beginnings of philosophy in India occurred in the remote past, probably before 1000 B.C.E.[8] From the start Indian philosophy speculated about the unity and the ultimate ground of the world. From the beginning philosophy developed in close connection with Indian religion—a connection that remains to this day.[9] Down through the years religion has nourished philosophy, and reciprocally philosophy has caused the development of religion from within. The earliest Hindu scripture, the Ṛgveda is credited with the philosophical assertion of the unity of the gods and the world. Dīrghatamas, the sage who arrived at and proclaimed this truth, is considered to be the father of Indian metaphysics. He may well have been the first in the world to think the fundamental thought: the one Being (*ekaṁ sad*) the wise call by various names (Ṛgveda I.164.46). Primordial being is the uncaused cause and sustainer of the world and all its diversity. On another occasion the Ṛgveda (X.129.2) attempts to explain the cause and ground of the universe without resorting to anthropological language: "What was there in the beginning? Nothing that can be named. 'That one (*tadekam*) breathed without breath, by its own inner power; than it, truly, nothing whatever else existed besides.'"[10] Whereas the first image from the Ṛgveda is more religious in nature, the second is more philosophical. Indeed the author of the second goes on to raise a doubt as to whether there is anyone who truly knows and can inform us about the why and how of creation. The author speculates that it is possible there was no creator and the world simply came to be by itself. Or, it is also possible that it may have had a creator or that it came out of nothing. Who can know? Certainly not the gods for they came into existence after the world. Thus a skeptical tension remains in this philosophical vision—a tension that refuses to resolve itself into a polarization on one side or the other.

In the Brahmaṇas, the next layering of Hindu scripture, philosophical speculation while still present is displaced by a focus on religious ritual. But the Brahmaṇas are followed by the Upaniṣads (800–600 B.C.E.)—philosophical dialogues between teachers and students that go back to earlier texts such as the Ṛgveda for their beginning insights. Scholars generally agree that the Bṛhadāraṇyaka is the oldest and most profound Upaniṣad. Yājñavalkya, its most eminent *rishi* or sage, speculates that the knowing subject is forever unknowable in conceptual terms. The self within, the pure knowing subject (*prājna ātmā*), is the only real that exists, and it has as its nature something like pure consciousness (*vijñāna*) and pure bliss (*ānanda*). These qualities, however, are not definitional but function merely as "pointers" to the Absolute Self that cannot be described. A second Upaniṣad, the Chāndogya, contains the great sentence "That Thou Art," which is interpreted as evoking an insight within the properly prepared student that each person's inner self (the *ātman*) and the absolute transcendental self (*Brahman*) are identical. One's true self (*ātman*), shorn of its empirical conditions and qualities, is nothing but the universal Self (*Brahman*). These empirical conditions and qualities that have to be removed or transcended are described as *karma*.[11] And these *karma* are the causes of rebirth that continues from one life to the next until the *karma* are removed. Removal of all *karma* results in the simultaneous revelation and realization of the true self as Brahman; and this, for the Hindu is the ultimate religious and philosophical goal. It is a goal, paradoxically, in which philosophy transcends itself. We can see then that these Upaniṣads have been the source for many of the basic religious and philosophical ideas that have developed over the centuries in India.

In addition to the Vedic-Upaniṣadic thinking just described, a second stream of philosophical thought existed in India. This tradition is represented by the Buddha's denial of self (*ātman*) and all that it implies. The Hindu systems based on the *ātman* doctrine of the Upaniṣads and the Buddhist philosophical schools based on the *nairātmya* or no-self doctrine of the Buddha conceive reality in two distinct and exclusive patterns. Whereas the Upaniṣads, and the Hindu schools drawing on them, conceive reality on the pattern of an inner core or self (*ātman*), immutable and identical amidst an outer region of impermanence, the Buddhists deny the existence of any immutable core and conceive of everything as being in flux. Existence for the Buddhist is momentary (*kṣaṇika*), unique (*svalakṣana*), and unitary (*dharmamātra*).[12] It is discontinuous, discrete, and devoid of complexity. All notions of continuing substance or self are illusory thought-constructions formulated under the spell of ignorance (*avidyā*) or wrong belief. The empirical outcome of such illusory belief in a self is ego-selfishness for material goods, sensuous pleasures, political power over others, and, worst of all for a philosopher, ego-attachment to one's own theories, thus rendering all thought corrupt.

Each of these streams of Indian philosophy, when carried to the extreme, denies the reality of the other. Hindu philosophy emphasizes the universal and the continuous to the exclusion of the changing and the different whereas Buddhist philosophy holds the opposite view. The Advaita Vedānta philosophy of Śaṅkara is the extreme exponent of the Hindu self or substance view and the Buddhist philosophy of Nāgārjuna represents the rejection of the Hindu view. Such an extreme polarization of philosophic positions invites the application of Derrida's corrective deconstruction. But this is not the only reason for bringing Derrida into contact with Indian philosophy.

Derrida as a Bridge between East and West

One part of the thesis of this book is that Derrida's philosophy provides a challenging and creative bridge between traditional Indian and modern Western philosophy. During the past century Indian philosophy has developed its own self-understanding by recasting its traditional systems in terms of the thought of Western thinkers such as Kant and Hegel. Modern Indian philosophy, although still incontestably Indian in that the traditional is still its basis, is also a product of some constructive interactions with powerful Western outlooks and ideas.[13] A strong example in this regard is the philosophy of K. C. Bhattacharyya.

A reclusive and abstruse thinker, K. C. Bhattacharyya (1875–1949) was a professor of philosophy at Calcutta University. His writings, though sparse, are considered to be profound and original. His originality came in the form of using Kant's Western philosophy as a challenge and stimulus to traditional Vedānta philosophy. Arapura says of Bhattacharyya, "his philosophy had an 'orientation to Kant' which meant arguing against the Kantian agnosticism pertaining to the knowledge of the self (the self being entertained by Kant only as a necessity of thought)."[14] By arguing against Kant from a Vedānta perspective Bhattacharyya also established a bridge between traditional Indian and modern Western philosophy. Bhattacharyya also engaged and disagreed with Hegel. Whereas Hegel absolutizes the Christian concept of spirit and subordinates all other philosophies and religions to it, Bhattacharyya rejects such an homogenization of viewpoints and instead establishes a system of dialectical alternation that leaves room for a valid plurality. In Bhattacharyya's view "Each experience by its self-deepening gets opposed to or synthesized with other experiences. One experience may enjoy another as a stage outgrown or in absolute conflict with it, where a third experience may emerge as adjusting them to one another."[15] Bhattacharyya completely repudiates the use of reason for interrelating religions or philosophies. Each position meets up with others by its own inner logic as it goes down deep into itself. The result is that the different positions when they are just let be systematize their mutual relations and consequently "present themselves in many alternative systems."[16] This view of "alternative absolutes" is fundamental to Bhattacharyya's philosophy and is his Indian response to Hegel's single "Christian" absolute.

To develop his theory of alternative absolutes, Bhattacharyya, in characteristic Indian fashion, resorts to negation.[17] Every system of philosophy or religion is seen to have its own logic and to be bound up with one of the fundamental views of negation.[18] The various kinds of negation "indicate certain distinctive temperaments or attitudes towards truth, certain familiar modes of handling a given content."[19] Bhattacharyya lists four types of negation: (1) that which involves no recognition of the need to control the faculty of "introspective attention";[20] (2) that in which the negation of negation "becomes not only definite but also positive";[21] (3) as a further development of the second, whenever "the original illusion which was pronounced subjective is turned objective, the given is taken to be the identity of the subjective and objective";[22] and (4) that in which "the first three views of negation may alternate."[23] In the end this means that "The absolute negation and the particular absolute affirmation are mutual negations in identity. This identity and this mutual negation are then the terminal points of all philosophy. Either side is beyond the dualism of definite truth and definite untruth."[24]

Bhattacharyya's philosophy has been recounted in some detail to demonstrate the creative development resulting from bringing together Kant and Hegel with traditional Indian philosophy in the first half of this century. The outcome of Bhattacharyya's engagement with the West is that no conclusion is reached. He leaves us with a new dialectic of alternatives, and basically this is still the position Indian philosophy finds itself in today. Into this context the engagement with Derrida, proposed in this book, comes as the possibility of promoting a new stage of development. Rather than being left in the position of the endless struggle between alternative absolutes (Bhattacharyya's outcome), the engagement of Indian philosophy with Derrida may provoke a deconstruction of these competing absolutes into a condition of ethical interrelationship. At any rate the new energy generated within Indian philosophy by Bhattacharyya's engagement with Kant and Hegel has been thoroughly exploited by subsequent thinkers (e.g., T. R. V. Murti in relation to Mahāyāna Buddhism[25]) to the point where it has now run its course and is being rehashed over and over again in books and Ph.D. theses that are no longer fresh or creative in nature. A new stimulus is needed.

As a potential new point of engagement for Indian philosophy with the West, Derrida offers several areas of interest. First is the fact that he shifts the focus from metaphysics to the philosophy of language. Interestingly, in one of his last public addresses, this was exactly the prescription for new life given to Indian philosophy by T. R. V. Murti. In his Presidential Lecture to the 1963 Indian Philosophical Congress, Murti argued that the time was ripe for Indian philosophy to rework itself from the perspective of the philosophy of language. This would have the beneficial effect, said Murti, of both recovering a vibrant strand of traditional Indian thought and building a bridge to the contemporary Western concern with language.[26] This book builds upon Murti's lead by suggesting that Derrida's philosophy of language would be a fruitful place to locate the Western end of this new bridge.

A second point of interest offered by Derrida is that, whereas Kant and Hegel stimulated Indian thought from a Christian religious context, Derrida is rooted in a different Western religious tradition, namely, Judaism. Susan Handelman in her book, *The Slayers of Moses,* effectively locates Jacques Derrida's philosophy in the context of Jewish rabbinic thought.[27] Whereas Greek thought is the source of Western logocentric metaphysics, Jerusalem is the source of an opposing stream of Western thought in which metaphor is seen as a logical statement (contrary to Aristotle)[28] and diversity, multiple meaning, and interrelationship are the goals to be realized.[29] Rather than an absolute unity of the kind presupposed in the Greek *logos* approach, rabbinic interpretation tends toward diversity. Rather than formulation of the relation between the general and the particular in classes, as in Greek logic, rabbinic thought views the general and the particular as interdependent. "The general is not an abstracted rule, but more of an extension of the particular, never losing its grounding in the particular; there is no fundamental opposition between them. These extensions and limitations are also never fixed, but fluid within the textual context."[30] Another point of emphasis within the Jewish tradition is that there is an inherent connection between language as Torah and the material world of nature. Unlike Greek thought that fosters subject-object separation and the development of an "objective science" as the way to understand the world, the rabbinic approach sees the interpretation of Torah as the way to unlock the secrets of creation. To understand creation one looks not to nature but to Torah. The Torah manifests the all-embracing underlying structure of reality—nothing is outside its scope. That is why Derrida maintains that there is no external referent, "There is nothing outside the Text."[31] Finally there is the rabbinic emphasis on the need for the written Torah to be accompanied by an oral Torah, without which the written is incomplete and incomprehensible. Because the role of the oral is the revelation of the deeper aspects of the written, the relationship between the two is not that of inferior to superior as in Greek thought. Rather the two are parts of one larger unity: the Torah has two parts, written and oral, and both are equally essential. And because the oral Torah presumes an act of speaking that requires the context of human relationship, it is therefore the case that Torah necessarily ends in the consideration of human relationships. All this is manifested strikingly in the ethical emphasis of the Hebrew prophets (e.g., Amos, Jeremiah, Hosea) and, as Norris has demonstrated, is also the goal of Derrida's philosophy of language.[32]

Whereas an earlier generation of Indian philosophers, led by Bhattacharyya, found needed stimulus in relating traditional Indian thought to Kant and Hegel and the Greek stream of Western philosophy, the time now seems ripe for Indian philosophy to engage the second stream of Western thought that flows forth from Jerusalem. Especially in the areas of the philosophy of language and hermeneutics, the modern West has found the stimulus offered by the rabbinic tradition to be rich and enlivening. The same result is very likely to occur in its engagement with Indian philosophy. The fostering of such an engagement is the aim of this book.

Chapter One

Philosophy East and West

Oh East is East, and West is West,
and never the twain shall meet,
Till Earth and Sky stand presently at
God's great judgement seat;
But there is neither East nor West,
Border, nor Breed, nor Birth,
When two strong men stand face to face,
though they come from the ends of the earth!

Rudyard Kipling—*The Ballad of East and West*

For centuries the philosophies of East and West have largely ignored each other. But the day is now dawning on serious attempts of Eastern and Western thought to relate, not in the form of caricatures of each other as has often been the case in the past but, in the words of Kipling, "as two strong men standing face to face, though they come from the ends of the earth." The willingness to work hard at taking each other seriously was evident at the recent "Sixth East-West Philosophers' Conference" held at the University of Hawaii in August 1989. Although the sixth such conference it was the first to include significant participants from Western philosophy. Scholars such as Richard Rorty, Alisdair

MacIntyre, Richard Bernstein, Ruth Ann Putnam, Hilary Putnam and Karl-Otto Apel all participated and seriously tried to understand Eastern philosophy on its own terms so as to find bridgeheads for philosophical dialogue between the two sides. The philosophy of science was one promising area that emerged. Another was the challenge to reason represented by Postmodernism along with discussions of "incommensurability in the Context of Pluralism." It was clear that all of these discussions were very much beginning attempts to find a common ground to bridge East and West—to locate problems on which the millennia of careful philosophical enterprise on both sides could effectively engage each other. Often there was frustration as scholars on one side or the other felt as if they were being bypassed like ships in the dark. The initial task for philosophers on both sides is to be willing to do the necessary homework of learning another tradition and its language, for often it is only through the subtleties of a thought-form embodied in its language that crucial nuances of the thought of others can be grasped. Only through the effort of "putting ourselves in the shoes of the other" and "seeing the world through the others eyes" can points of possible contact be seen and serious East-West philosophy be begun. This book is one such beginning attempt, taking as its point of contact the philosophy of language.

In his essay "Philosophy as a Kind of Writing," Richard Rorty suggests that there are two traditions of philosophy, which exist in a state of constant rivalry—philosophy as a rational dialogue in the quest of communicable truth versus philosophy that rejects the goal of rational consensus and thrives on techniques of paradox and style (philosophy as "writing" in Rorty's sense).[1] This "writing" approach in philosophy contains within itself a serious skepticism regarding the ability of the philosophy of reason to attain ultimate truth. Much German and French philosophy clearly falls into Rorty's "writing" tradition. So also does much Eastern philosophy. On both sides a good deal of the debate has proceeded within the context of the philosophy of language. One Western thinker who has pushed the "writing" critique of language to the limit (as perceived in the West) is the French philosopher Jacques Derrida. It has been observed that Derrida's encounters with other Western philosophers of the opposing rationalist tradition, thinkers such as Austin and Searle, are really nonencounters.[2] The distance between their perspectives seems simply too great to be bridged. By contrast, when Derrida's thought is put together with the philosophies of some of the great Indian philosophers, thinkers such as Bhartṛhari, Śaṅkara, Aurobindo, and Nāgārjuna, we find significant grounds for mutual engagement. It may well be the case that Eastern philosophy as a whole relates more easily to the "writing" rather than to the "rational" tradition of Western philosophy. That suggestion, however, remains to be tested. The more limited purpose of this book is to critically compare Derrida with the Indian thinkers Bhartṛhari, Śaṅkara, Aurobindo, and Nāgārjuna in regard to the limits and function of language.

We will restrict our comparison of Derrida with the East to Indian philosophy, although realizing that very fruitful results would likely obtain from a study of Taoism[3] and Chinese and Japanese Buddhism. However there is an advantage in not try-ing to assimilate too many Eastern perspectives at once. Consequently we will restrict our comparison of Derrida to Indian philosophy, and there to three Hindu and one Buddhist thinkers. Although this leaves out several other important schools of Indian philosophy, it provides a representative sampling of the main approaches to the philosophy of language within the Indian tradition. At some future point Jaina philosophy, especially its *anekānta-vāda* or "no one view" philosophy,[4] could be fruitfully taken up for comparison with Derrida. The remainder of this chapter attempts to introduce each of the thinkers dealt with by briefly setting them in their own contexts.

The Philosophical Context of Jacques Derrida

Because of their early dates (c. 2nd to 8th century c.e.), and the lack of concern for biographical details in classical India, we have little reliable knowledge of the personal details surrounding the lives of Nāgārjuna, Bhartṛhari, and Śaṅkara. To be consistent we will not attempt to delve into the personal backgrounds of Aurobindo, a contemporary Indian philosopher, or Derrida. This suits Derrida well. Derrida admits that his early experience of extreme isolation as the child of a Jewish family during a period of persecution and racial violence emphasized his sense of belonging to a marginal and dispossessed culture.[5] However he maintains that these early influences have no causal relationship to his philosophy. Christopher Norris does observe, however, that Derrida's early experiences become relevant to his writings only "insofar as they take the form of a relentless interrogation of philosophy by one who—for whatever reason—shares rather few of philosophy's traditional beliefs."[6] Yet it is also clear that Derrida sees himself and his work as part of the Western philosophical tradition. Norris observes that, in Derrida's critique of Levinas and Foucault, his essential point is that "Deconstruction can have no *critical* purchase on the texts of Western logocentric reason if it thinks to move decisively 'beyond' tradition by a leap on to different ground."[7] There is no doubt however that Derrida deeply challenges at least one stream of the Western philosophical tradition, those who ground themselves within the parliament of reason. A. J. Ayer, for example, dismisses Derrida as a mere rhetorician and literary gadfly whose ideas are not worth the attention of serious philosophers.[8]

Derrida clearly belongs within Rorty's "writing" stream of Western philosophy. Norris, however, convincingly demonstrates that, contrary to popular opinion, Derrida does not play fast and loose with reason but rather values it sufficiently to want to test it with the toughest challenge. "Who is more faithful to reason's call, who hears it with a keener ear . . . the one who offers questions in return and tries to think through the possibility of that summons, or the one who does not want to hear any question about the principle of reason?"[9] Norris also makes a good case to show that Derrida's thought does not end up in playful nihilism, as is frequently assumed, but rather has a strong ethical dimension. Part of Derrida's criticism of Western philosophy is that it has become so preoccupied the epistemological problems of truth and reason that it no longer can effectively be a bridge from the thinking through of these problems to the practical sphere of ethical action. At this point Derrida's Jewish background may be showing through, for it is chiefly in his Jewish writings that this concern for ethical response appears.[10]

In his book of readings on Deconstruction, Mark Taylor helpfully situates Derrida with regard to his philosophical heritage. Derrida comes at the conclusion of a line that begins with Kant and runs through Hegel, Kojève, Husserl, De Saussure, Kierkegaard, Nietzsche, Wittgenstein, Heidegger, Sartre, Merleau-Ponty, Levinas, Bataille, and Blanchot.[11] In Taylor's analysis the crucial point comes with Heidegger who, fully persuaded that metaphysics has run its course, asks what and how we are to think after the end of philosophy? Heidegger answers that the task remaining is to try to think what philosophy has left unthought. As Taylor puts it:

> The task of thinking is, then, to think the unthought that answers the question of how there can be presence as such. Heidegger defines this unthought as "the *difference* between Being and beings," or, more concisely, "difference *as* difference." In attempting to discover the Being common to all particular beings, metaphysics fails to ask how this grounding presence can itself be present.[12]

This focus on "difference" is given further support in the comment of Levinas against Hegel's Greek view of self-fulfillment as a case of metaphysical identity, "as the auto-affection of self-consciousness."[13] Rather than self-constituting by an identity relation, Levinas argues that the subject is constituted by an other, over which it has no control, ultimately Yahweh, the divine Other—constitution by difference rather than identity. Blanchot shifts this experience into the realm of literature, of writing. The present, he argues, can never be captured in writing, for writing, like all art is always of the past. Thus time prevents our experience of identity with art by insinuating an irreducible absence in the midst of all presence. "With the recognition of the impossibility of presence, the space of time becomes the time of space."[14] Taken together the spacing of time and the timing of space open an interval that Blanchot defines as *"la difference."* There is no spatial or temporal continuity or identity as in *logos* theory—there is only spatial and temporal disjunction (difference). Difference is the disjunction that beginninglessly disjoins from itself and in so doing prevents any experience of unity. Taylor concludes:

> Blanchot's *différence* becomes Derrida's *différance* —one of "the unheard-of-thoughts" with which Derrida tries to think "beyond absolute knowledge" by rethinking Nietzsche's and Heidegger's difference. . . . Like Heidegger, Derrida responds that philosophy does not, indeed *cannot,* think difference. But for Derrida, as for many others, Heidegger's difference is insufficiently different from the difference of metaphysics. Along with writers like Sartre, Merleau-Ponty, Levinas, Bataille, and Blanchot, Derrida attempts to think the unthinkable by thinking difference as difference and other as other.[15]

The preceding outline presents, not Derrida's thought (for that is the function of the following chapters), but the context in which his thought occurs. This context, with its debate between identity and difference crowned by the need to somehow go beyond both, is not unfamiliar to Indian philosophy.

The Indian Philosophical Context

Indian philosophy begins with the Hindu scripture, the Vedas (c.1500–500 B.C.E.). The various schools of Indian philosophy are frequently divided into two groups, those who base themselves upon the Vedas (the *āstika* schools), and those who establish their position in rejection of the Vedas as revealed truth (the *nāstika* schools). Of the thinkers we will examine Bhartṛhari, Śaṅkara, and Aurobindo may be taken as representative of Hindu *āstika* schools, while the Buddhist Nāgārjuna comes from a *nāstika* school. In addition to the Buddhists, other Indian schools that reject the Vedas include the Jainas and the materialistic Cārvākas. For the Western philosopher not familiar with Indian philosophy a clear presentation of these various schools with a critical assessment of each can be found in P. T. Raju, *Structural Depths of Indian Thought.*[16] For an approach that treats the same schools in terms of specific philosophical problems see Karl H. Potter, *Presuppositions of India's Philosophies.*[17] In terms of the issues of identity and difference discussed with regard to Derrida's context, we could say that the Hindu philosophers Bhartṛhari, Śaṅkara, and Aurobindo begin with the Vedic perspective, which may be generally termed one of "identity," whereas Nāgārjuna's Buddhist thought may be broadly characterized by "difference." However we shall see that each of these thinkers tries in his own way to overcome the philosophical problem of the identity-difference dualism yet still retain his own fundamental insight.

An important aspect of each of the schools of Indian philosophy is that they regard themselves as *darśanas* or ways of viewing the world that must include a pathway to liberation or release. In Indian thought philosophy cannot be regarded as merely theoretical knowledge. If that knowledge does not also somehow transform one's everyday life in such a way that liberation is realized, then it is invalidated as a philosophy. Indian philosophy in this regard is more like the wisdom traditions of the West. This requirement, however, does call to mind one of the points of criticism that the deconstruction tradition of Western philosophy mounts against epistemology and metaphysics; namely, that the latter has become so focused on reason that it can no longer relate to the practical problems of daily life. Such a result would be unacceptable, it appears, both to Derrida's deconstruction and to the requirements of Indian philosophy. As a *darśana* or particular way of seeing reality, each school of Indian philosophy offers its own answer/prescription/pathway to release.

But release from what? The schools of Indian philosophy agree that in our ordinary experience of life we are immersed in an ignorance or *avidyā* that pervades all of our perception and thinking thus preventing us from experiencing life and the world as it is. This ignorance not only causes us much suffering, due to our misperception of reality and our unclear selfish thinking, but, for most schools, it prevents us from escaping this misery at death by causing us to be reborn to go through yet another round of *avidyā* tainted experience until we die only to be reborn yet again. This process, technically termed *saṁsāra,* has been going on beginninglessly and will continue until, with the awakening provided by one of the schools, we are enabled to see things as they are and are thus released from entrapment in *avidyā* or ignorance. This release is the freedom, enlightenment or liberation that is the goal of all the Indian philosophers we will examine. They will differ radically, however, in the way that goal is conceived and in their prescription as to the means by which it may be realized. In this study our particular focus is on status and role of language in the thought of these Indian philosophers when compared with language in Derrida.

In the Hindu scriptures, the Vedas, speculations on the nature of language began very early.[18] In the *Ṛgveda,* thought to be the earliest, several hymns are devoted to Speech (*Vāk*) and the same trends continue in the later *Brāhmaṇas* and *Upaniṣads*. Speech is said to permeate all creation and to be identified with the divine. The *Ṛgveda* states that there are as many words as there are manifestations of Brahman.[19] The *Āraṇyakas* and early *Upaniṣads* continue to equate Speech and Brahman. As one *Āraṇyaka* states, the whole of Speech is Brahman.[20] In the *Taittirīya Brāhmaṇa* Speech is seen as the support of all creation.[21] Various symbols are used to indicate the divine nature of Speech and its evolution to form the world. Prajāpati and Speech are viewed as male and female copulating to create the world.[22] Murti puts it well when he says, "The Brahmanical tradition stemming from the Veda takes language as of Divine origin (*Daivī Vāk*), as Spirit descending and embodying itself in phenomena, assuming various guises and disclosing its real nature to the sensitive soul."[23]

In the *Upaniṣads* speculations on language become

more philosophical. Brahman is defined as the one reality without a second and is identified with Speech.[24] The *Māṇḍūkya Upaniṣad* links the unspeakable absolute with the speakable through speech itself. It creates the symbol AUM, which incorporates the three levels of consciousness—waking, dreaming, and deep sleep—and reaches out beyond the transcendent where sound itself comes to an end. Brahman, which is said to be Speech is also said to be AUM.[25] Just as leaves are held together by a stalk, so all speech is held together by AUM.[26] In both the *Upaniṣads* and the *Ṛgveda* speech is seen to have various levels ranging from the manifoldness of the phenomenal words to the absolute oneness of Brahman as *Vāk*.[27] The implication is that only as we perceive language at its higher levels do we get a clear revelation of its meaning. Thus it is said that the ignorant person seeing and hearing speech in its overt manifest forms does not know its real nature. To the wise only does language reveal its intrinsic nature. The ordinary person caught in *saṁsāra* is lost in appearances and fails to penetrate to the deeper reality that the language of scripture reveals.

The Sāṅkhya-Yoga, Mīmāṁsā, Vedānta, and Grammarian schools of Indian philosophy are not only loyal to this Vedic tradition but give it further development. The Buddhists, however, reject this tradition of linking language with scripture and the divine. Bhartṛhari is the leading systematic philosopher of the Grammarian school. He stays closest to the scriptural view of language in that for him *Vāk* or Speech is directly identified with Brahman or the divine, the scripture is seen as the criterion manifestation of *Vāk* as Brahman and language as providing the means by which that divine may be realized to reach release or *mokṣa*. Śaṅkara, a leading philosopher of the Vedānta school, agrees with seeing scripture as revelation and thus necessary for the realization of Brahman, but rejects Bhartṛhari's complete identification of language with Brahman. For Śaṅkara scripture and all language ultimately must be transcended for Brahman and release (*mokṣa*) to be realized. Auro-bindo, a contemporary Indian philosopher, does not fit exactly into any of the classical schools of Indian philosophy. Aurobindo is probably closest to the viewpoint of Bhartṛhari and the Grammarian school. But Aurobindo separates himself from Bhartṛhari and the other classical Indian thinkers by introducing a modern Western evolutionary perspective into his theory of language. As a Buddhist, Nāgārjuna rejects the Vedic identification of language with the divine. For Nāgārjuna language is not divine in any way but is conventional. Nor is there a special category of language called scripture that can provide a revelation of reality that is otherwise unattainable. Words, even those of the Buddha, must be tested in one's own personal experience before being accepted. But even the words of the Buddha, like all of language, are infected with a subject-object duality that must be overcome if one is to be liberated from *saṁsāra*. For Nāgārjuna release (*nirvāṇa*) requires an escape from or a going beyond our ordinary entrapment in language and its distorting *avidyā* of subject-object duality.

With this brief introduction, let us now proceed to our comparative studies of Derrida and Bhartṛhari (Chapters 2 and 3), Derrida and Śaṅkara (Chapter 4), Derrida and Aurobindo (Chapter 5), and Derrida and Nāgārjuna (Chapter 6).

CHAPTER TWO

DERRIDA AND BHARTṚHARI'S *VĀKYAPADĪYA* ON THE ORIGIN OF LANGUAGE*

PROFESSOR T. R. V. Murti, in his 1963 presidential address[1] to the Indian Philosophical Congress, presented a challenge to Indian philosophy—a challenge that seems to have fallen on deaf ears. Murti challenged the traditional schools of Indian philosophy to rethink themselves and their relationships with one another from the perspective of language. Not only would this breathe fresh air into the stale situation obtaining in Indian philosophy—because the Kantian and Hegelian reinterpretations of basic Indian metaphysics had about run their course—it would also allow a significant engagement between Indian philosophy and the contemporary Western concern with the philosophy of language. This chapter takes up that challenge by entering a dialogue between traditional Indian philosophy as formulated by Bhartṛhari and the modern Western

---

*First published in *Philosophy East and West,* vol. 40, no. 2 (1990).

deconstructionist thought of Jacques Derrida. In approaching this dialogue I will follow the insightful suggestions of Professor Murti as to one point on which this dialogue should be focused, namely, the issue of the origin of language.

THE ORIGIN OF LANGUAGE

Attempts have been made both in Western and Indian thought to derive language from nonlinguistic sources such as bodily gestures,[2] interjectional sounds,[3] imitative sounds, etc., and to argue that convention was used to further evolve such naturalistic beginnings. Although Professor Murti did not speculate at length on the origin of language, he did situate the question clearly within its two extreme views: language as somehow always being present, as being a priori; or language as being a convention created by human beings. Murti, following Cassirer in the West and Mīmāṁsā in India, maintains that language is a priori. Against the argument from convention (*saṅketa*) where the relation between words and their meanings are created by either humans or by God, Murti agreed with the Mīmāṁsā view that words and their relation with meaning are eternal, underived, and impersonal.[4] Convention presupposes language. To make conventions people must already possess words. But this is clearly circular, says Murti, and he points to the eternal and beginningless nature of language. "An absolute beginning of language is untenable. Linguistic usage is continuous."[5] In India the Buddhist discovery of the constructive role of the subject in knowing challenged the view of language as eternal. From the Buddhist perspective, language expresses merely imaginary constructions (*vikalpa*) that play over the surface of the real without ever giving us access to it. All language, including even the Vedic language, is merely a human construction. Although useful for daily affairs, language can give us no knowledge of the real. These two opposing Indian views of the origin of language find some quite surprising links with the contemporary Western language debate—particularly in the deconstructionist "Grammatology" of Jacques Derrida.[6]

Like the Buddhists, Derrida cannot accept the idealizing of language that has often typified traditional thought. Like the Buddhists, Derrida focuses his analysis on the role of the subject in linguistic experience. But in his analysis he also finds much that is compatible with the Vyākaraṇa viewpoint as systematized by Bhartṛhari. Because Vyākaraṇa is at many points a defense of Mīmāṁsā doctrine, the apparent bridging of the Buddhist and Mīmāṁsā poles in Derrida's analysis may well offer some new insights into the Indian philosophy of language. At the very least, engaging Derrida's thought will provide a new forum from which Indian philosophy can constructively engage with the modern Western philosophy and literary criticism.

Derrida speaks from a long and complex Western heritage. It is a heritage from which he seeks to disengage because it has been encapsulated by the idealized pole of logocentricism—language as an a priori experience of divine presence. In his analysis Derrida cites, among many others, Plato, Aristotle, Kant, Hegel, Husserl, Heidegger, Nietzsche, Marx, Saussure, and Rousseau. A masterful and concise survey of how Derrida relates to and draws from these thinkers has been offered by Christopher

Norris and will not be rehearsed here.[7] For our purpose we will focus on Derrida's analysis and critique of Saussure and Rousseau.[8]

Derrida begins by pointing out that in the traditional logocentric view "The beginning word is understood, in the intimacy of self-presence, as the voice of the other, and as commandment."[9] As Aristotle saw it, voice and breath have an immediate relationship with the mind that naturally reflects the divine *logos*. Between *logos* and mind is a relationship of natural signification—the mind mirrors things by natural resemblance. Between mind and speech there is a relationship of conventional symbolization. Spoken language is a first conventional symbolization of the inner reflection of the *logos*. Written language is a second, further removed convention. As the first convention voice or speech is closest to the reflected presence of the thing itself. Written words are always secondary and technical representatives of speech. Speech being closer to the reflected *logos* has a stronger sense of both the meaning signified and the action naturally evoked. Writing, being a further step removed, has a weakened sense of both meaning and implicit commandment.[10]

From this perspective then, writing is definitely downgraded. This was already evident in the thought of Socrates as reported by Plato in the *Phaedreus*. Socrates argues that contrary to expectations, writing does not improve one's memory and wisdom but in fact accomplishes the reverse: memory will suffer because people will begin to rely on writing—writing will not impart wisdom to the mind but rather will only serve as a reminder; by learning things through writing people seem to know much, whereas for the most part they know nothing; using writing is not real teaching for the students become filled, not with wisdom, but with the conceit of wisdom, and as such they will be a burden to their fellows.[11] Socrates also objects to writing because of the way it objectifies wisdom, and the negative possibilities that open up: "Once a thing is put into writing, the composition... drifts all over the place, getting into the hands not only of those who understand it, but equally of those who have no business with it. And when it is ill-treated and unfairly abused, it always needs its parent to come to its help, being unable to defend or help itself."[12] Thus, in the classical Western view the oral, already one step removed from the real, is not only the parent of the written, but must constantly be pressed into service to interpret and defend the written. The origin of language is located in speech, which symbolizes the clear mental reflection of the divine. Writing is a step further away from the divine and, being a representation of a representation, experiences a loss of meaning and power. All of this is very close to the traditional Vyākaraṇa viewpoint in which the spoken Veda is the real word mirroring Brahman. It is through the spoken Veda that *dharma* or duty is known, and it is by chanting Vedic mantras that karmic ignorance may be removed. Writing has, perhaps, an even lower status than it is given by Socrates. Writing in the Vedic Sanskrit tradition is for those who are too dull to remember. Writing can never perfectly represent all the nuances of the spoken word and is therefore always secondary. To the Prātiśākhyas (the rules for prosody, phonetics, accentuation, and *sandhi*) fell the task of ensuring that the spoken words of the Vedas were preserved and passed on in their pristine form.[13]

For both the Greek and the Vyākaraṇa viewpoints then, language originates from a natural reflection of the divine that is symbolized first at the level of speech and secondarily at the much lower level of writing. Although convention is involved in the formulation of both speech and writing, such conventions are totally dependent on the *logos* or the natural reflection of the divine in the mind for both their meaning and power. Due to its transcendental origin, language is understood in both of these traditions to be, at base, divinely given. Equally important for Derrida, is the fact that such logocentric approaches locate the essence at the interior, closer to the breath and voice than to writing, which is exterior.

In his discussion of Saussure and Rousseau, Derrida shows that they too follow the classic logocentric pattern. Both end up valuing the interior of language as essence, staying within the logic of identity and the ontology of presence.[14] Derrida engages in a thorough critique of this view of language not to cause it to self-destruct in favor of the opposite pole—language as an exterior, which is unable to engage the real, the Buddhist position—but to find a way out of the polarized debate altogether. This he does through clues picked up first from Saussure and later from Rousseau. Derrida does not make the Buddhist move of treating language as *vikalpa* or mere imaginary constructions. Rather he makes the surprising move of seeing the origin of language in writing—a writing that is both exterior and interior. Derrida makes this move in the hope of escaping the ontology of presence and the ethics good and evil that such an ontology necessitates. The problem of stating his view of the origin of language so as to avoid falling back into the error of metaphysics is something Derrida thinks he manages "only by a hairsbreadth." His method, he says, is to borrow the resources of his own position from the logic it deconstructs—and in so doing finding a positive foothold.[15] In this, of course, he differs from the Buddhist philosopher Nāgārjuna[16] who deconstructs ontology, not to get a foothold from which to make statements about the real nature of language, but rather to demonstrate its ultimate *śūnya* or lack of any such "footholds." Derrida's use of Rousseau's notion of an originary force or trace of "writing" may well bring him closer to Bhartṛhari than to Nāgārjuna, with whom he has been previously identified.[17] It will raise afresh the question as to whether Derrida's deconstruction of the origin of language really does allow him to escape metaphysics by a "hairsbreadth" as he claims. In examining Derrida's deconstruction let us look first at the beginningless nature of language and second at its pregnant quality (with time as midwife) that allows it to continually sequence itself.

Language as Beginningless (*Anādi*)

The problem of asking the question of the origin of language is that it must be asked within already existing language. We cannot get outside of language to examine its origin. Thus to attempt to think the origin of language is to arrive at a paradox that cannot be resolved. Derrida's sustained study of the origin of language takes the form of a commentary on Rousseau's "Essay on the Origin of Languages." This commentary provides the main substance of the second half of Derrida's *Of Gram-*

matology. In his reading of Rousseau Derrida examines the significance of Rousseau's own metaphors and arguments for the theory he purposes.[18] Indeed Derrida states his own tactic as being a kind of literary-philosophical judo—to use "the strengths of the field to turn its own strategems against it."[19] The aim, however, is not a simple reversal of categories or poles of argument—the outcome and method of traditional metaphysics—but rather the undoing of both a given order of priorities and the system of conceptual opposition that makes such an order possible. This aspect of Derrida's approach is very parallel to the Catuṣkoṭi or "Four Pronged Negation" method of Nāgārjuna.[20] But his outcome is different. Rather than seeking to reduce critical thought to silent meditation, Derrida concludes with positive statements about "writing" as the dynamism or originary force in all language.[21]

That Rousseau cannot possibly mean what he says in his "Essay on the Origin of Languages" is the outcome of Derrida's perversely literal reading of Rousseau's text. Rousseau argues that speech and song originate together in the natural unity of the inarticulate cry.[22] Primitives neither sing nor speak but simply emit muted bellowings that their wants draw from them. The first cries of young children are similar. In the transcending of need by desire and the awakening of pity by imagination the primitive cry is modulated into speech. In his *Dictionary of Music* Rousseau defines a song as a modification of the human voice.[23] In speech accents are seen as but imitative modifications of the voice of song. Therefore, for Rousseau, languages carrying more accent, for example, Italian, are closer to song and the primal source of speech. The differentiations from unitative cry to song to speech and finally to writing (an imitation of speech) are seen by Rousseau as a descending hierarchy marked by an increasing loss of the good originary presence reflected in the initial cry.[24]

Derrida's analysis of Rousseau's *Essay* demonstrates that the modifications that are the birthpangs of song and speech have the very characteristics of separation and sequencing that Rousseau takes to typify degeneration of the word. "What emerges is the fact that language, once it passes beyond the state of primitive cry, is 'always already' inhabited by writing, or by all those signs of an 'articulate' structure which Rousseau considered decadent."[25] By *writing* Derrida refers to any separation of the unitary cry into different parts. Rousseau's natural cry, characteristic of the unity of nature and identity of origin, is somehow "shaped and undermined by a strange difference which constitutes it by breaching it."[26] The origin of language is due to nothing but the differences of articulation and structure that characterize language as it is experienced. Thus, argues Derrida, Rousseau's description of the point of origin as a unitary or undifferentiated cry of pure presence cannot be accepted. Even Rousseau "unconsciously" seems to recognize this when he introduces the notion of a special "supplement" that "both signifies the lack of a 'presence', or state of plentitude for ever beyond recall, and *compensates* for that lack by setting in motion its own economy of difference."[27] Derrida fastens onto this "unconscious admission" by Rousseau as revealing the true nature of language. It is not a hierarchy of degradation descending from a "fallen" or "breached" state of original plentitude. Rather it is the beginning dynamic of difference that is characteristic of all levels of writing, speech, and thought. Rousseau's artifactual supplement is identified by Derrida as revealing the originless nature of language. Rousseau is unable to conceive of language and society except in terms of difference.

The shift from originary presence to originless difference has significant implications for the privileging of speech over writing—which has characterized much of traditional Western and Indian philosophy. But before turning to examine those implications in Chapter 3, let us pause and compare Derrida's analysis of the origin of language with that offered by Bhartṛhari. The prima facie reason for undertaking such a comparison is that Bhartṛhari, like Derrida, sees the necessity of a *continuity* between the originary state and the manifested experience of language. Bhartṛhari in common with the Mīmāṁsā, the Yoga, and Vedānta schools of Indian philosophy, see language as beginningless[28]—this is parallel to Derrida's view of language as originless. And like Derrida, Bhartṛhari makes use of time as the sequencer or cause of articulated (differentiated) speech.

LANGUAGE AS SEQUENCED-DIFFERENTIATED BY TIME (*KĀLA*)

Against Rousseau and all theories of creation by convention, Derrida asserts that language has no origin. But he does maintain that language at all levels is pregnant with a force toward separation or difference. The different parts or separations that characterize the written text are from the same dynamic that manifests itself in spoken words. In his analysis Derrida is attempting to recover what is already present in language; thus Derrida's often misunderstood statement, "There is nothing outside the text."[29] Just as the dynamic of difference (separation, articulation) is beginninglessly present in the written text, so it is also present in speech. There is no metaphysical "other" outside of text or speech that starts language. This insight of Derrida's is nicely paralleled by Bhartṛhari's view that the dynamics of separation into word (*śabda*) and meaning (*artha*) is beginninglessly present in language at all its levels[30]—from the uttered or fully sequenced speech (*vaikhari vāk*) to the apparently unitative intuition (*paśyantī vāk*) in which sequencing is present only as a pregnant force. Between these two levels, says Bhartṛhari, is the mental speech (*madhyamā vāk*) with its thought separation into sentence meanings and sounds that have not yet been uttered. Bhartṛhari, like Derrida, sees sequencing or difference as the characteristic dynamic of language in all its levels. Even the innermost apparently unitative level of speech is pregnant with the power of difference. As Bhartṛhari puts it in his *vṛtti, paśyanti vāk,* though it is One, has the power to produce sequence within it.[31] There is no pure presence or *logos* devoid of this pregnant power. For Bhartṛhari the one Brahman is the *Śabdatattva* or Word-Principle. *Śabdatattva* is not a lesser Brahman, a mere *upāyah,* but is identical with Brahman itself, the only Brahman there is.[32] For Bhartṛhari, Brahman, as the Word-Principle, is an intrinsically dynamic and expressive reality, and the Universe as a whole is to be understood as its manifestation under the form of temporal becoming. Both Bhartṛhari and Derrida describe this immanent power of becoming in terms of time and space.

For Bhartṛhari it is through the power of time

(*kāla*) and space (*dik*) that the one Brahman appears as many. (*Kāla* and *dik* are not different from Brahman but are those aspects of Brahman that allow manifested sequence to come into being.) For example, when time sequences appear as differentiated objects, then time as a power seems to be different from Brahman, but really it is not.[33] It is striking that Derrida's key term *différance,* which for him is the essence of language, is described in terms of the coincidence of meanings in the verb *différer:* to differ (in space) and to defer (to put off in time). Thus *différance* for Derrida invokes both space and time as essential to the origin of language.[34] Bhartṛhari's wisdom in naming both space and time as the powers of Brahman by which language occurs is highlighted in Derrida's critique of structuralism. Structuralism, he says, focuses on space and reduces time to a dimension of space. Derrida, like Bhartṛhari, finds it necessary to avoid the simple choice of one of the terms over the other—his goal is to break with the classical philosophical system of metaphysical oppositions.[35]

In his critique of Husserl's phenomenology, Derrida notes that time functions as an endless deferring of presence that drives yet another paradoxical wedge into the ability to experience pure presence.[36] What we experience is not the pure presence of logocentric metaphysics but a dynamic temporal becoming. Bhartṛhari would seem to agree when he describes time as the sequencer that puts off the pure experience of presence by differentiating things into states of birth, existence and decay. Two illustrations are offered by Bhartṛhari to make clear this meaning. The power of time in the creative process is like that of the wire puller in a puppet play.[37] Just as the wire puller is in complete control of the puppet play so *Kāla* has full control over the sequencing of language. Ordinary cause and effect processes cannot operate unless *Kāla* infuses them with life force. This control of cause and effect by time is further illustrated in relation to the strings a hunter ties onto the feet of small birds that he uses as bait for larger ones. The small birds can fly over a limited distance but they cannot go beyond the length of their strings. Like the strings controlling the movement of birds so the words of language are controlled by the "string of time." Derrida describes this temporalization of language as the movement of *différance*.[38] This intrinsic movement of *différance* permits the articulation of speech and writing and founds the metaphysical opposition between signifier and signified, expression and content. For Derrida *différance* or articulation originates in the experience of space and time.[39]

For both Derrida and Bhartṛhari the origination of language in the differing forces of time and space accounts for our experience of past, present, and future. Derrida's analysis picks up on a comment from Saussure that "*what is natural to mankind is not spoken language* but the faculty of constructing a language."[40] This inherent impulse to construct language is named a *psychic imprint* or *trace* by Derrida and would seem to parallel Bhartṛhari's illustration of the yolk of the peacock's egg. For Bhartṛhari language has within itself a dynamic presence pregnant with the power of differentiation. Bhartṛhari likens this pregnant power to the energy (*kratu*) in the yolk of a peacock's egg, that, though one, has an actionlike function and assumes the sequence of its parts.[41] Derrida uses the term *trace* to refer to this psychic imprint, because of its rooting in the past, which causes us to experience it as an "always-already-there."[42] Derrida calls the trace an *absolute past* to distinguish it from our ordinary use of *past*. As he puts it, "if the trace refers to an absolute past, it is because it obliges us to think a past that can no longer be understood in the form of a modified presence, as a present-past."[43] The trace is not simply a passive past for it proclaims as much as it recalls—it has impulsive force, the force of articulation or differentiation. Thus, although our concepts of past, present, and future result from the articulation force of the trace, these concepts taken alone are not exhaustive of the trace. The essence of the trace is a dialectic "of protention and retention that one would install in the heart of the present instead of surrounding it with it."[44] The dialectic of the trace is what Derrida calls *différance*. It proclaims as much as it recalls. Therefore it is in dynamic relationship with past, present, and future. It is the absolute ground out of which they arise.[45]

Bhartṛhari's conception of the driving force inherent in the absolute Word-Principle (*Śabdatattva*) bears many similarities to Derrida's analysis. Comparing Bhartṛhari with Derrida helps us to locate significant differences between Bhartṛhari and Śaṅkara that have been frequently missed by previous commentators such as Gaurinath Sastri[46] and K. A. Subramanian Iyer[47], both of whom offer a decidedly Advaitic reading of the *Vākyapadīya*.[48] In addition, an understanding of Derrida awakens us to points of close contact between Indian and modern Western thought on the nature of language.

Bhartṛhari views time as a power independent of all speech objects, yet also inherent in them, pushing them through successive stages. Rather than the passive external superimposition of the successive changes upon Brahman, the Advaita model in India, and the logocentric model in the West, the image in Bhartṛhari is one of urgent changes through pregnant forces that constitute the essence of the absolute itself (*Śabdabrahman*). In *Vākyapadīya* 3:9, verse 14, we find Bhartṛhari's position clearly stated:

> By means of activities similar to the turning of the water-wheel, the external and all-pervasive Time turns out (*kalayati*) all the fragments (*kalāḥ* objects) and thus acquires the name of *kāla* (Time).[49]

Like the everrenewed pushing or lifting up of water by the waterwheel, so the all-pervading and all-penetrating Time drives or pushes (*kalayati*) all things, releasing them from their material causes and making them move. This is why time is given the appropriate name of *Kāla*.

The distinction between Bhartṛhari's conception of *Kāla* and the Advaita Vedānta view of *māyā* is not with regard to locus of *Kāla* or *māyā* in Brahman (for both schools seem to agree on this), but rather with regard to the ontological power ascribed to *Kāla* or *māyā*. Bhartṛhari's *Kāla* doctrine emphasizes the driving (*kalayati*) power inherent in Brahman that is the first cause of the bursting forth of the worldly phenomena. The Advaita conception of *māyā,* although it does indeed (in the Vivarana tradition, at least) locate *māyā* in Brahman,[50] does not seem to attribute to *māyā* the same degree of ontological "pregnancy" or "driving force" as Bhartṛhari ascribes to *Kāla*.

Although it is acknowledged that *māyā* has two aspects, obscuring (*āvaraṇa*) and projective (*vikṣepa*), the stress in Advaita interpretation seems to be on the former more than the later. For the Advaitin, the focus is upon *māyā's* obscuring of Brahman; for Bhartṛhari, the projective power or driving force of *Kāla* occupies center stage. Whereas this difference may at first appear to be merely a question of difference of emphasis, a definite difference seems to appear when the ontological status of the phenomenal projection itself is analyzed. Whereas for Advaita the projected world of *māyā* is neither real nor unreal but inexplicable (*anirvacanīya*), the *Kāla*-driven world of Bhartṛhari, although increasingly impure as it becomes manifested as worldly phenomena, never looses its direct ontological identity with Brahman. The relation between the phenomenal world and Brahman for Bhartṛhari is continuous and does not have the mysterious break of an "all or nothing" sort that both Śaṅkara's *māyā* doctrine and the classical Western philosophy of being or presence require. Whereas superimposition (*adhyāsa*) is a fitting term for Śaṅkara,[51] it does not seem appropriate to Bhartṛhari or Derrida. The illustrations offered in the *Vākyapadīya* are dynamic images: of Brahman busting forth in illumination (*sphoṭa*), of pregnancy (the peacock egg producing all the colors of creation), and of a driving force like the pushing-up or lifting-up action (*kalayati*) of the waterwheel.

Helārāja's *Tīkā* on *Vākyapadīya, Kāṇḍa* 3, *kārikā* 9:62 makes clear that there are three ontological levels in Bhartṛhari's thought: Brahman, his Powers of Time and Space, and the diversity of phenomena.[52] Once again this contrasts with Śaṅkara's Advaita and Western logocentric philosophy. For

Śaṅkara there is only one ontological level, Brahman, with *māyā* as an epistemological second level (which is neither real nor unreal but inexplicable). For Bhartṛhari the highest ontological level is Brahman as *Śabdatattva* (without manifest sequence). It is called *paśyantī,* which also indicates the direct and full perception of meaning; thus the culmination of our experience of our *vāk* or word.[53] Although Time is inherent in Brahman at this stage, no sequence has yet occurred—it is still pure potentiality. The next ontological level, in descending order, is *madhyamā.* At this level *Kāla* begins to push or drive delimited portions of Brahman into sequence. This it accomplishes with the help of *prāṇa* or breath. In our experience of language this corresponds to the separation of the unitary *sphoṭa* into the mental sequence of thoughts. The full blown appearance of diversity appears when Time has released all the secondary cause-effect relations that have been waiting as stored-up memory traces (*saṁskāras*) or "seed-states" in all the cycles of the universe. In this third or *vaikharī* level the power of Time as the sequence evidenced in ordinary cause-effect relations is fully experienced. To return to Bhartṛhari's own analogy, at this stage we see the birds on time's strings flying about to the full extent of the limits that their "strings" allow. Time is thus the governing power of all thought objects in the universe. It is time that drives or pushes objects into action to the point where their own secondary cause-effect relations take hold. But also the behind-the-scene activity of time controls the extent of the secondary actions of objects and their moment of decay or withdrawal.

The constructive power of time is also encountered in Derrida's explanation. Derrida's deconstructive approach seeks to recover what is already there.[54] What is already there in the *différance* that is the essence of language is a dialectic of protention and retention that provide the opposing dynamics of our experience of the present.[55] Protention is the dialectic of the present with the anticipation of the future. Retention is the dialectic of the present with memory of the past. The present has no existence apart from these two dialectics of time. In Derrida's rather complex thought these two dialectics of future and past are seen as implying each other:

> in the undecomposable synthesis of temporalization, protention is as indispensable as retention. And their two dimensions are not added up but the one implies the other in a strange fashion. To be sure, what is anticipated in protention does not sever the present any less from its self-identity than does that which is retained in the trace. But if anticipation were privileged, the irreducibility of the always-already-there and the fundamental passivity that is called time would risk effacement. . . . Since past has always signified present-past, the absolute past that is retained in the trace no longer rigorously merits the name "past." . . . the strange movement of the trace proclaims as much as it recalls: *différance* defers-differs [*diffère*].[56]

If I understand Derrida, our experience of the present is constituted by a dynamic mixing of anticipations of the future and memories of the past—all experienced as a simple moment of the present. Past and future constitute the present not by dividing it up, but by being in dynamic tension with each other.[57] Derrida's thinking here has striking similarity with the Buddhist view that there is no present time (*vartamānakāla*) apart from past and future. The present has no meaning except in relation to past and future.[58]

Bhartṛhari (*Vākyapadīya* vol. 3, ch. 9, v. 4) uses similar notions in his discussion of time: permission (*abhyanujñā*) and prevention (*pratibandha*). The function of Time called permission (*abhyanujñā*) allows things to be born and to continue in existence.[59] By its other function, prevention (*pratibandha*), Time obstructs the inherent capacities of objects, and "old age" is then experienced. In this way the stages of life and the seasons are ordered. When Time is functioning under its impulse of prevention, decay or *jarā* occurs. *Jarā* (decay) and growth (*krama*) operate like pairs of opposites. When *jarā* is active, *krama* or growth is blocked, and vice versa.[60] But the underlying substratum of all of this activity is the driving impulse of Time.[61] Time remains eternal although the actions of growth and decay come and go.

As a result of the activity of growth and decay, Time that is one, attains the states of past, present, and future. Thus, when an action ceases, Time, conditioned by that action, is called *past*. When something is about to happen, Time, conditioned by that event, is called *future*. When action has been initiated but is not yet completed, Time is then called *present*.[62] In this way the one transcendent reality Time is experienced, through the actions of the secondary causes it releases or restrains, to be sequenced into past, present and future. Time says Bhartṛhari, is like the everflowing current of a river that deposits some things on the river bank and at the same time takes away others.[63]

So it is that the seasons change, as symbolized by the motions of the sun and stars. As Helārāja puts it, "The seasons may be looked upon as the abode of Time, because it appears as the seasons. The power called 'Freedom' of Brahman is really Time and it appears diversified as the different seasons like Spring, etc."[64] Thus the appearance of the Universe, which is really without sequence, as something with sequence, is the work of Time.[65] All of this squares very nicely with Derrida's description of the temporalization of language as play—not play "in the world," but play as the free becoming of language itself.[66] To use Bhartṛhari's terms, it is the free phenomenalizing of the *Śabdatattva* itself, not the action of a separated God "playing" in the world. Nor is it a play of *vikalpa* as Buddhism would have it, a play of human imagination that has no touch with the true nature of the world. Derrida's play as the free becoming of language and Bhartṛhari's play of the *Śabdatattva* are reality itself!

In another analogy, past, present, and future are said by Bhartṛhari to be like three paths on which objects move without any confusion.[67] Helārāja's comment makes an analogy of this view with the Sāṅkhya-Yoga explanation of Time found in Vyāsa's *Bhāṣya* on *Yoga Sūtra* III:13. Here the activity of Time is equated with the ever present movement of the *guṇas* on the three paths of being (*adhvā*). The notion that objects and mental states do not all occur simultaneously due to the prevention and permission activity of time is clearly stated. The psychological mechanism involved is that of inherent tendencies or memory traces (*saṁskāras*), which sprout like seeds when the conditions created by the everchanging *guṇas* are favorable.[68] The point of this parallel between Sāṅkhya-Yoga and Grammarian doctrine is to show how the three apparently conflicting qualities can coexist in harmony. As Helārāja puts it,

> Just like the three ingredients, having the characteristics of serenity (*sattva*), activity (*rajas*) and inertia (*tamas*), though existing simultaneously due to their eternity, acquire the subordinate and principal relation and effect beings through their peculiar evolution, in a proper manner in the splendour of their own course of action, so also, these (three) time-divisions, by the magnificence of their own power (become) capable of effecting sequence in external aspects.[69]

The past and the future hide objects so they are like *tamas* or darkness (says Bhartṛhari). The present enables us to see the objects and so it is like light or the *sattva* of the Sāṅkhyas. *Rajas* stands for the activity of Time itself.[70] For both Sāṅkhya-Yoga and the Grammarian, the harmonious coexistence of objects on the three paths of time makes the ordered sequence of the world possible. Time, like an eternal road, is the substratum on which the objects of the world come and go. The road, like time, always remains the same.[71]

Conclusion

It is remarkable that thinkers so separated in time and place should have given such similar explanations of our experience of language. Both Bhartṛhari and Derrida see time, as the sequencing of language, to be its basic character and its constituting source. Both enter into this deep discussion of time in relation to the absolute and the origin of language, not as a fascinating metaphysical aside, but to explain how the unitary Word manifests itself in experience as the diversity of speech and writing—without recourse to an external other (God or *logos*). For both language is not logocentric, as it is in Western classical philosophy or in the Advaita Vedānta of Śaṅkara, nor is it empty of reality, as Buddhism maintains. Language, for Derrida and Bhartṛhari is a dynamic becoming that is itself the very stuff of our experience of reality.

There are, of course, some very definite differences between Derrida and Bhartṛhari—such as Bhartṛhari's *pratibhā* notion of a direct perception of the word itself (the *sphoṭa*), which Derrida would completely reject. But that will be dealt with in Chapter 3.

CHAPTER THREE

DERRIDA AND BHARTṚHARI ON SPEECH AND WRITING*

A QUESTION suggested by Professor T. R. V. Murti in his 1963 presidential address focused on the status of the spoken word within language.[1] Murti points out that for Indian thinkers, language was primarily the spoken word or speaking itself (*vāk*). However, this definition of language does not identify it with the overt sounds produced physiologically or with the written signs that are merely phonetic copies of the spoken sounds. In fact, said Murti, "the distinction between *śabda* (Word) and *dhvani* (Sound) is basic to the Indian philosophy of language. To identify them, to take the physical sound as the word, is a *category mistake*."[2] With this contention Jacques Derrida agrees. It is Derrida's contention that virtually the whole of Western metaphysics from Plato to Rousseau and Lévi-Strauss have made the category mistake of identifying language or *logos* with the spoken word.[3] But whereas

*First published in *Philosophy East and West,* vol. 41, no. 2 (1991).

for Murti the category mistake was in taking the outer sound instead of the inner word to be the essence of language, Derrida makes the utterly surprising move of seeming to go in the opposite direction—of identifying the essence of language with writing. Although Murti was challenging naturalistic schools of philosophy such as the Buddhists, Derrida confronts the logocentric position (which Murti represents) as well as the Buddhists. For when Derrida describes language as "writing" he not only means that writing is prior to the spoken reflection of the inner *logos*, but also that language is not merely a sort of external speaking or writing as the Buddhists suggest. What Derrida attempts is a deconstruction or self-analysis of language that exposes the mistake of a reductionism in either direction: inward to the divine *logos* or outward to the conventional sign. In his desire to escape all philosophical oppositions such as "inner" versus "outer," Derrida subtly states his position: "language is not merely a sort of writing 'but' a possibility founded on the general possibility of writing."[4] For Derrida, as we shall see, "writing" characterizes both the "inner" and the "outer" word in dynamic interrelationship, which, at points, bears striking similarity with the Indian philosophy of language put forth by Bhartṛhari in his *Vākyapadīya.*[5]

Indian philosophy has been even more emphatic than Western thought as regards the priority of the oral over the written. The tradition in both Hindu and Buddhist philosophy has been to correct the written text with the oral. It is the oral word, carefully memorized, guarded by the discipline of the *Prātiśākhyas,*[6] and passed down from teacher to student through succeeding generations that has remained authoritative in India.[7] Thus Derrida's proposition that writing is prior, not secondary, to speech will seem at first blush to be quite incredible. Even the West, with its greater stress on the written, has generally accepted the historical priority of oral language to writing and so finds Derrida's thesis to be outrageous. However, recent research by André Leroi-Gourhan on the marks associated with cave paintings and by Alexander Marshack on the possibility of calendrical markings on prehistoric bone implements, in the discovery of the Tartaria Tablets, raises fundamental questions about our dating of the invention of writing to Sumer, 3100 B.C.[8] Derrida cites this evidence as an initial reason as to why we should take him seriously. But his real point has nothing to do with the historical priority of the written. His proposition that writing is prior to speech is simply part of his Nāgārjuna-like tactic of exposing the weakness of a position by turning its own strategems against itself.[9] By reversing the usual speech-writing hierarchial opposition, which has obtained in the West since Socrates and throughout Indian thought, Derrida's ultimate aim is to counter the simple choice of one of the terms over the other—to escape the system of metaphysical opposition that has dominated much Western and Indian philosophy. "Writing" for Derrida is not just the inscription of words on paper or computer program, but includes the neuronal traces in the brain that Freud identifies as memory[10] and indeed is the active moment of differentiation that is the creative force of all language.[11] Derrida even playfully alludes to DNA as a "writing" or trace present in all living substances. Writing and its originary trace begins to sound like the *saṁskāras* or originary memory traces of traditional *karma* theory. Derrida's initial aim in all of this is to deconstruct the traditional priority accorded speech (and its logocentric metaphysics of presence) over writing.

In relating Derrida's critique to Indian philosophy and, in particular to Bhartṛhari, we will examine Derrida's deconstruction of the logocentric priority of speech over writing; language as manifested in Derrida and Bhartṛhari; and language as a means for spiritual realization.

DERRIDA'S DECONSTRUCTION OF THE PRIORITY OF SPEECH OVER WRITING

Derrida follows Nietzsche and Heidegger (and perhaps implicitly Nāgārjuna in Indian philosophy) in elaborating a critique of "metaphysics" by which he means not only the Western philosophical tradition but everyday thought and language as well. "Western thought, says Derrida, has always been structured in terms of dichotomies or polarities: good vs. evil, being vs. nothingness, presence vs. absence, truth vs. error, identity vs. difference, mind vs. matter, man vs. woman, soul vs. body, life vs. death, nature vs. culture, speech vs. writing."[12] These opposites, however, have not been seen as equal entities. The second term is always put in the position of being a fallen or corrupted version of the first. Thus evil is the lack of good, absence is the lack of presence, error is a distortion of truth, and difference is an obstruction of identity. The two terms are not held in an opposing tension but are placed in a hierarchial order that gives the first term priority both in time and quality. The general result has been the privileging of unity, identity, and temporal and spatial presence over diversity, difference, and deferment in space and time. Thus Western philosophy (and much of Indian philosophy) has answered the question of the nature of being in terms of *presence*.

Within this broad context Derrida's critique of Western metaphysics focuses on the privileging of the spoken over the written word. As we have already noted, this same privileging of speech over writing has characterized Indian thought. Barbara Johnson, one of Derrida's translators, clearly summarizes his analysis of the privileging of speech as follows:

> The spoken word is given a higher value because the speaker and listener are both present to the utterance simultaneously. There is no temporal or spatial distance between speaker, speech, and listener, since the speaker hears himself speak at the same moment as the listener does. This immediacy seems to guarantee the notion that in the spoken word we know what we mean, mean what we say, say what we mean, and know what we have said. Whether or not perfect understanding always occurs *in fact,* this image of perfectly self-present meaning is, according to Derrida, the underlying ideal of Western culture.[13]

Derrida calls this belief in the self-presentation of meaning *logocentricism,* from the Greek *logos* (speech, logic, reason, the Word of God). Writing, from the logocentric perspective, is seen as a secondary representation of speech to be used when speaking is impossible. The writer puts thought on paper, distancing it from the immediacy of speech and enabling it to be read by someone far away, even after the writer's death. All of this is seen as a corruption of the self-presence of meaning, an opening of meaning to forms of corruption that the presence of speech would have prevented.[14] Derrida's critique is not aimed at reversing this value system, and showing writing to be superior to speech. Rather, his critique attempts to dissect the whole system of metaphysical opposition upon which the speech versus writing debate is grounded. In so doing Derrida finds that both speech and writing are beginninglessly structured by difference and distance. The very experience of meaning is itself an experience of difference, and this difference is shown by Derrida to inhabit the very heart of what appears to be immediate and present. In his commentary on Freud's "mystic writing-pad" Derrida shows that difference is present even in the structures of the unconscious.[15] The apparent experience of a unitary self-presence of meaning and consciousness is found to arise from the repression of the differential structures from which they spring.[16] Logocentricism deconstructed is shown to depend on difference, and difference, in both time and space, to be characteristic of speech as well as writing.

Before examining Derrida's deconstruction of logocentricism in detail, let us see if there are schools of Indian philosophy that fit into the logocentric category and are thus subject to Derrida's critique. Within the *āstika* or orthodox traditions certainly the Sāṁkhya-Yoga, Vedānta, and Nyāya schools are structured in terms of polarities such as identity versus difference, soul or self versus matter-*māyā,* truth versus error, etc., in which the second term of the pair is always of a lower status. Ontological Being–Presence–Consciousness is identified with the first term of the pair. All also venerate speech over writing, perhaps even more strongly than is the case with Western philosophy. There is also a valuing of phonetic speech and writing over nonphonetic languages, such as Chinese. Pāṇini's *Aṣṭādhyāyi* or Grammar is based on the sound of spoken Sanskrit[17] and is thus a prime candidate for what Derrida calls *phonocentricism,* which is open to all the criticisms of logocentricism.[18] The negative status given to writing in the West is paralleled and accentuated in the Indian tradition. Scribes in India have had a low status and the texts they write are judged to be very unreliable. The written is valued only as a teaching aid for those too dull to remember. In fact the very act of writing was held to be ritually polluting in a late Vedic text—the *Aitareya Āraṇyaka* 5.5.3 states that a pupil should not recite the Veda after eating meat, seeing blood or a dead body, having intercourse, or engaging in writing.[19] Clearly the *āstika* or orthodox schools of Indian philosophy (with the exception of the Grammarian school, which will be discussed later) largely share the same logocentric biases toward Being and Speech and against writing as those located by Derrida in Western metaphysics. Nor do the *nāstika* or heterodox schools escape Derrida's net. Jainism strongly shares in the soul-matter dialectic and like Buddhism agrees that language is merely conventional and cannot touch the real. This separation of speech from the real (most extreme in the Mādhyamika negation of speech into silence) is attacked by Derrida as being just as unsatisfactory as the extreme logocentric position, with its identification of speech with the real. It is not just the logocentric view, which Derrida criticizes, but any philosophy that privileges one opposite or extreme over the other. Derrida's net of deconstructive critique would then seem to be as potentially devastating to Indian philosophy as it is to Western philosophy. The one school that may escape Derrida, by having prefigured much of his critique, is the Grammarian school, especially in its formulation by Bhartṛhari. Let us now test out this suggestion as we examine Derrida's deconstruction of logocentricism.

Both Derrida and Bhartṛhari agree that, since philosophy must be done in language, literary analysis is as important and perhaps more important than logical analysis. As Derrida puts it, philosophers have been able to impose their various conceptual systems only by ignoring or suppressing the disruptive effects of language.[20] Bhartṛhari in *Vākyapadīya* I:14 describes Grammar as the "purifier of all the sciences." It is through the use of correct forms of language—as identified by the Grammarians—that philosophic or any other kind of knowledge can be obtained. Both Bhartṛhari and Derrida break down the barrier between literary criticism and philosophy.

If all knowledge comes through language, is there a source or ground of language outside of or beyond language? Does language depend on something else—God, the *logos*, Brahman? The answer for both Derrida and Bhartṛhari is "no." In Bhartṛhari's *Vākyapadīya* the Absolute is the *Śabdatattva*, the Word-Principle, and therefore is not something apart from or beyond language. Derrida establishes his "no" by deconstructing the viewpoint that has dominated metaphysics; namely, that a separate Being or Presence is immediately reflected in speech and then given a secondary representation in writing. Derrida deconstructs this argument as it is presented in Plato, Rousseau, and others, by finding writing, when understood as *différance,* to contain all of spoken language, and all inscribed language. This of course requires an enlarged concept of writing. In his reading of the *Phaedrus,* Derrida locates the basis for such an enlarged view of writing in Plato's own text. Whereas Western philosophy has seen writing in the *Phaedrus* as an orphan unable to communicate knowledge, Derrida finds evidence for a second kind of writing in 276a of the *Phaedrus:*

> Socrates: But now tell me, is there another sort of discourse that is brother to written speech, but of unquestioned legitimacy? Can we see how it originates, and how much better and more effective it is than the other?
> Phaedrus: What sort of discourse have you now in mind, and what is its origin?
> Socrates: The sort that goes together with knowledge, and is written in the soul of the learner, that can defend itself, and knows to whom it should speak and to whom it should say nothing.
> Phaedrus: Do you mean the discourse of a man who really knows which is living and animate? Would it be fair to call the written discourse only a kind of ghost (eidolon) of it?
> Socrates: Precisely . . . [21]

In this passage Derrida finds evidence for a deconstruction or reversal of the usual Platonic view of writing: "While presenting writing as a false brother—traitor, infidel, and simulacrum— Socrates is for the first time led to envision the brother of this brother, the legitimate one, as another sort of writing: not merely as knowing, living, animate discourse, but as an inscription of truth in the soul."[22] This other sort of writing, written on the soul of the learner, is called the *trace*[23] or *arche-writing*[24] by Derrida, and it is seen as the dynamic source of both speech and external writing. The necessity of arche-writing or trace being composed of the movement of difference is established in Derrida's analysis of another dialogue, *Philebus* (17 a–b). Here Socrates notes that although the sound or cry we first speak is one, it also possesses an unlimited variety of different sounds.[25] Only through a limiting and mastering of the differences is understanding obtained. Difference and relation are irreducible, says Derrida, and are designated as "writing" by Plato.[26] Derrida, goes on to observe that all of this wisdom of Socrates, though originally spoken, comes to us only because it is written down after his death.

Derrida also establishes the need for the inner trace or arche-writing by a critique of Saussure's linguistic theory. For Saussure, the basis of language is found in the natural bond of the signified (concept or sense) to the spoken word of which the written image is a contamination.[27] But Saussure suggests that language can be best understood by an analogy to both the form and content of writing. Saussure finds that "difference" is the source of linguistic value.[28] It is precisely this general movement of difference, says Derrida, that is the arche-writing or trace that contains within it the possibility for all oral and written language. Speech and writing are expressions of one and the same language. Arche-writing is nothing but dynamic, expressive *différance*. It does not depend on sound or writing, but is the condition for such sound and writing. Although *it does not exist,* its possibility is anterior to all expressions (signified-signifier, content-expression, etc.). This intrinsic *différance,* concludes Derrida, permits the articulation of speech and writing, and founds the metaphysical opposition between signifier and signified. *Différance* is therefore the formation of form and the being imprinted of the imprint.[29]

Instead of the term *arche-writing* or *trace* Bhartṛhari uses the term *Śabdatattva* or *Word-Principle.*[30] Brahman, the Word-Principle, is without beginning or end. Although proclaimed to be one, it is divided by the function of its inherent powers. In particular through the sequencing power of time (*Kāla*) the Word-Principle manifests itself in the expressive activity of language, which becomes the model for all other activity.[31] This activity is seen as a real manifestation and not as a merely apparent (Śaṅkara's understanding of *vivartate*) activity. Bhartṛhari states, "Knowers of tradition (the *Vedas*) have declared that all this is the transformation [*pariṇāmah*] of the word. It is from the *chandas* [hymns of the Vedas] that this universe has evolved."[32] "Here the term *pariṇāmah* is used to describe the same process which is described in I.1 by *vivartate.*"[33] Writing at the end of the fifth century A.D., Bhartṛhari does not speak in terms of causalty such as typify Śaṅkara's later debates, but emphasizes the marvelous activity by which the multiple universe is manifested out of the one Word-Principle or *Śabdatattva.*[34] For our present purposes the important point is that for Bhartṛhari, Brahman, as the Word-Principle, is an intrinsically dynamic and expressive reality, and that language (and all of the universe) is its manifestation through the process of temporal becoming.[35] Like Derrida, Bhartṛhari also uses the notion of a beginningless trace that is inherent in consciousness. Unlike Derrida, however, Bhartṛhari discusses the trace of speech in relation to previous births. "This residual trace of speech has no beginning and it exists in every one as a seed in the mind. It is not possible that it should be the result of the effort of any person. Movements of the articulatory organs by children are not due to instruction by others but are known through intuition."[36] Iyer notes that *pratibhāgamyā* or the residual trace of speech here stands (1) for the residual traces of language use in previous births, (2) for the faculty of speech with which the child is born, and for the child's instinct toward activating these traces in human life situations.[37] The next verse makes clear that such instinctual traces are inherently involved in all cognition for "There is no cognition in the world in which the word does not figure. All knowledge is, as it were, intertwined with the word."[38]

As was the case for Derrida, Bhartṛhari sees the inherent trace consciousness of language as conditioning all psychic experience from deep sleep to dreams to ordinary awareness and even to mystical states (states in which there is a direct supersensuous perception of the meaning-whole or *sphoṭa*). In the dream state, says Bhartṛhari, the only difference is that the seeds or traces of language function in a more subtle manner.[39] It seems evident that Derrida's development of Freud's thought would be easily accommodated within Bhartṛhari. Just as Derrida finds the psychological mechanism behind the Western experience of an unchanging *logos,* presence, or Self to be the suppression of the experience of difference within the psyche, so Bhartṛhari rejects other Indian schools who equate the experience of Self with something external to consciousness and language. "[The Self] exists within in every individual, but appears to be external."[40] For Bhartṛhari, and it would seem for Derrida, the experience of Self is the unobstructed experience of *Śabdatattva* or arche-writing manifested in the temporal dynamic of language. Obstacles to this experience are identified as the incorrect understanding and use of language forms and the "ego-knots" such impure usage produces.[41]

Not being part of the Western debate over the opposition between speech and writing as sparked by Socrates in the *Phaedrus,* Bhartṛhari gives only passing reference to the status of writing—and then only to identify texts whose authors are known as opposed to texts considered to be without an author (*apauruṣeya*). When he does refer to writing, as in *Vākyapadīya* I:132, Bhartṛhari uses the term *āgama.* In his review of this verse and others where *āgama* is used, Iyer concludes that what is meant is simply a text composed by some writer in contrast to *śruti* or Vedic texts which are said to be without authors. The contrast is not between written and spoken—as is the case for Derrida—but between texts whose authors are known and texts considered to be without any author.[42] Although the Vedas may be written, they are, like consciousness, eternal and so do not depend on any human author.[43] They are the criterion manifestation of the *Śabdatattva* and do not depend on being written down by any human author for their preservation. For those who cannot see the meaning of the Vedas, the composing of commentaries, through the use of reason that divides up the unitary meaning of the sentence, is done for teaching purposes or for the benefit of those who can see only superficially.[44] Bhartṛhari, however, agrees with Derrida that one benefit of *āgama* is that when the teacher or author dies, their words continue and serve as the seed basis for the formation of further tradition.[45] Overall, there is no doubt that texts composed by authors and authorless speech are both manifestations of the *Śabdatattva* for Bhartṛhari. For both, however, the temporal transformation of the originating source of language through speech and writing is seen to be continuous. If Bhartṛhari were here today, and able to understand Derrida's thought, perhaps he would not find the term arche-writing too far from his *Śabdatattva.* Certainly both would find common cause against those who locate the absolute outside of language or who maintain that language has no purchase on reality.

Language as Manifested in Derrida and Bhartṛhari

For both Derrida and Bhartṛhari it is the pure possibility of difference that is manifested as language. The intrinsic *différance* of the arche-trace permits the articulation of speech and writing. The arche-trace manifests into the opposing forms of inner concept and outer sound image. Derrida uses the technical term *sign* to refer to the whole, *signified* to refer to the abstract concept, and *signifier* to refer to the spoken and heard sound image.[46] Bhartṛhari's technical terminology would seem to provide a virtually perfect parallel: *sphoṭa*[47] to indicate the whole, *artha* to refer to the concept or meaning, and *dhvani* to refer to the uttered and heard sound. For both Derrida and Bhartṛhari the linguistic whole (the sign or *sphoṭa*), has an inherent force toward differentiation that produces the double manifestation of inner meaning (signified, *artha*) and spoken sound (signifier, *dhvani*). Although sign and *sphoṭa* are irreducible, neither can be experienced as pure presence. Rooted within language, even in its most holistic form, is the pregnant push towards sequencing, spacing, punctuation—differentiation in time and space. In the *Vākyapadīya,* the *Śabdatattva,* symbolized by the seed sound *AUM,*[48] is sequenced by the power of time into the various recentions of the Veda and all spoken words.[49] For Derrida the image is one of the sign, as the linguistic whole, differentiated by spacing (on the page) and interval or pause (in speaking) into articulated meaning and sound image. The actualizing of this inherent force for differentiation enables language to function. But it is, at the same time, the limit of language. As Derrida puts it, since a sign (the unity of signified and signifier) cannot be produced within the plentitude of absolute presence, there is, therefore, no full speech, no absolute truth or full meaning.[50] In the words of Lao Tzu, "The tao that can be spoken is not the eternal tao."[51] Or as Hegel once put it, "When *speaks* the soul, alas, the *soul* no longer speaks."[52] But whereas Lao Tzu and Hegel are mourning the inability of manifested language to make present the soul or the *tao,* Derrida and

Bhartṛhari emphasize the positive contribution of articulated speech. The *sphoṭa* and the sign (Derrida's whole) are manifested, and in the dynamic tension of that manifestation lies truth.

Rather than arriving at a skepticism of language, namely that it is devoid of any truth content (the conclusion of the Buddhists and many modern skeptical critics of language), truth is seen to be contained in the very dynamics of language itself. Thus Derrida's thesis that there is no referent outside of the text is not as nihilistic as it sounds at first, and Bhartṛhari's *sphoṭa* is not as artificial an entity as much Indian philosophy has assumed.

In *Vākyapadīya* I:5, there are two terms that Bhartṛhari uses to describe the Veda: it is the *prāptyupāya* or the means for the attainment of Brahman; and it is the *anukāra* or symbolization of Brahman. For now let us confine our attention to the term *anukāra* which comes from the root *kṛ*, "to do" or "to make" and suggests the dynamic activity of the Word-Principle. The *Vṛtti* elucidates the verse by stating that the activity of the Vedic seers in speaking the *mantras* is the criterion case of word-making activity. The term *mantra*, notes Aurobindo, signifies a "crossing over" through thought (root *man*, "to think", and *tṛ* "to cross over") from the Absolute or Unmanifested to the human experience of manifested language.[53] As pure Sanskrit language, the *mantras* are conjunctions of certain powerful seed syllables that induce a particular rhythm or vibration in the psychosomatic structure of consciousness and arouse a corresponding psychic state. Such seed sounds can be differentiated in a great variety of ways producing an immense progeny of language. The evocative power is at its height before the *mantras* become too locked into particular forms of articulation. Poetry is at its peak before language becomes too fully elaborated. Then it must be deconstructed or evolved backward to recover its original power for signification. Articulation is necessary but the further it goes the greater is the loss of freedom and power within language.

This also seems to be what Derrida means when he refers to the prose book as a corpse of language that must be exited from or transcended[54]—the delimiting of the multisignificant roots has been pursued to its logical conclusion, and the power of the word has been exhausted. The aim of the project of deconstruction, says Derrida, agreeing with Aurobindo, is to get back to metaphoric, poetic language where the power for signification has not yet been used up.[55] Bhartṛhari also reminds us that, as language divides and separates, this necessary process in the end can become a source of confusion. The process of difference, pushed to its logical conclusion, produces such a plethora of speaking accents that communication of knowledge is obstructed.[56] Unlike Derrida and Aurobindo, Bhartṛhari's solution is not to deconstruct or reverse the process of differentiation, but to control it by the imposition of strict grammatical rules (the science of the Grammarians) by which the power of the root *mantras* to convey knowledge and action will not be obfuscated.[57] Bhartṛhari, along with the other Grammarians, claims to have uncovered the pure forms of the correct unfolding of the patterns of differentiation inherent in the *Śabdatattva* and symbolized (*anukāra*) in criterion form in the initial speaking of the Vedas.[58]

Another aspect of the meaning of *anukāra,* as we

find it in *Vākyapadīya* I:5, is the notion of resemblance. Carpenter puts it well:

> The Veda, as the *anukāraḥ* of Brahman, standing in a position of imitative resemblance to its source, occupies a mediating position between this source and the diverse forms of the world. It presents, within the dynamic framework of the world as a whole, a level of expression and action which is directly related to the unitary ground of that world. It thus presents the established order of *dharmaḥ* in contrast to the often disorderly world of everyday experience (*vyavhāraḥ*).[59]

The Veda is not a direct description of Brahman, the *Śabdatattva*. Language functions to mediate action, not ideas. The verb not the noun is basic. Vedic revelation, for Bhartṛhari, does not provide us with a representation of the transcendent object, the Word-Principle. What the Veda does is to mediate the inherent action of the *Śabdatattva* directly through the dynamic idiom of language. "The Veda is thus the outward linguistic form of the dynamic self-manifesting act of the Word-Principle itself."[60] To the extent that other language use approximates the Veda, it also shares in the self-manifesting of the Word-Principle. The function of the Grammarians is to help all language use, from whatever science, realize that goal.[61]

It seems clear that Derrida would not agree with Bhartṛhari's privileging of scripture in general or the Veda in particular. He would probably also criticize the notion of the Veda as manifesting the original linguistic form or *anukāra* of arche-writing. The critique Derrida offers of the Bible as a Grammar of Being in accordance with which "the world in all its parts is a cryptogram to be constituted or reconstituted through poetic inscription or deciphering."[62] has yet to be tested against the Veda—but that is another project. It is clear, however, that Bhartṛhari's emphasis on language as active rather than passive, as necessarily engaging both thought and action, as not representing but mediating the absolute, is largely in agreement with the overall thrust of Derrida's deconstructive critique.

Language as a Means for Spiritual Realization

If language is experienced as a mediation of arche-writing or *Śabdatattva,* then it is also a means for spiritual realization. Language is not merely epistemological in function. Over against Śaṅkara's assessment of *māyā* (including all language and even the Vedas) as having epistemological but not ontological status,[63] both Derrida and Bhartṛhari locate the real in arche-writing or *Śabdatattva,* which is not separate from manifested language. Although for Śaṅkara language (and the Vedas) must be transcended for spiritual realization (*mokṣa*), for Bhartṛhari it is in language that union with the *Śabdatattva* is realized.

Before looking at Bhartṛhari's clear conception of *Vāk* or speech as the means for the spiritual realization (*prāptyupāya*) of *Śabdatattva,* let us test Derrida's Grammatology to see if, like Bhartṛhari's science of Grammar (*Vyakāraṇa*), it can also be construed as a means for spiritual realization. In his deconstruction of the Western metaphysics of *logos* or Presence, Derrida takes pains to distance himself from any suggestion of theistic religion.

Derrida considers his own notion of arche-writing or prototrace to be an atheistic or, more properly, a nontheistic proposal. Of course the term *arche-writing* is meant to be confounding. How can a writing or trace precede the writing or trace that is left behind? But aside from Derrida's perplexing play of language with regard to the divine, we do find some hints that support our interpretation of arche-writing as parallel to *Śabdatattva*. In *Of Grammatology*[64] Derrida discusses the nature of arche-writing or trace. The manifested trace cannot be thought without thinking of the retention of difference, of all manifestation, so that the trace contains all history and all possibility. This history and possibility is not static but contains an inherent force for unmotivated self-manifestation.[65] This self-manifestation is structured according to the diverse possibilities—genetic and structural—of the trace. "This formulation is not theological, as one might believe somewhat hastily," says Derrida. "The 'theological' is a determined moment in the total movement of the trace."[66] The theological is a historically second dissimulation of the trace. The general structure of the unmotivated trace is that of temporal becoming. The trace is not more natural than cultural, not more biological than spiritual. "It is that starting from which a becoming-unmotivated of the sign, and with it all the ulterior oppositions between *physio* and its other, is possible."[67]

Derrida's writing is purposely not systematic. But he does give a fair hint as to the shape that the becoming of the trace takes:

> Representation mingles with what it represents, to the point where one speaks as one writes, one

> thinks as if the represented were nothing more than the shadow or reflection of the representer. . . . In this play of representation, the point of origin becomes ungraspable. There are things like reflecting pools, and images, an infinite reference from one to the other, but no longer a source, a spring [source]. There is no longer simple origin. For what is reflected is split *in itself* and not only as an addition to itself of its image. The reflection, the image, the double, splits what it doubles. The origin of the speculation becomes a difference. What can look at itself is not one; and the law of addition of the origin to its representation, of the thing to its image, is that one plus one make at least three.[68]

It is the direct experience of this dynamic process of becoming, not as a process of static reflection or metaphysical opposition, that would for Derrida be the realization of the spiritual whole. The sensitive deconstruction of the illusions of permanence, of stasis, or presence (which our ordinary experience and many of our philosophies have superimposed on the becoming of language) is Derrida's prescription as the means for the realization of the whole. We cannot name this whole *spiritual* for that is already to engage the vocabulary of metaphysical opposition. But to understand the whole as manifestation of the inherent *différance* of the trace is for Derrida the goal. To go from the inscribed trace (writing) to the spoken word and the arche-writing that prefigures and predisposes both, only to be thrown back again, in a continual deconstructive reverse, would seem to be Derrida's use of language as a spiritual discipline. Although this may look like a Mādhyamikan answer, it is not. The deconstructive reverse does not result in the silence (*śūnya*) of language, but rather in the realization that the dynamic tension in the becoming of language is itself the whole. For Derrida, all of this cannot be understood as abstract theorizing. The language we are deconstructing is our own thinking and speaking—our own consciousness. We ourselves are the text we are deconstructing. That is why, for Derrida, there is nothing outside of texts. Deconstruction is the process of becoming self-aware, of self-realization.

Can we say that this Derridean deconstruction of language is a means for spiritual realization? A comparison of Derrida with Bhartṛhari helps us to see why we can answer this question in the affirmative. Like Derrida, Bhartṛhari maintains that the analysis of linguistic experience is an examination of the very nature of our consciousness. Just as for Derrida consciousness is nothing but trace or writing, so for Bhartṛhari consciousness is nothing but *Śabdatattva*—the inextricable intertwining of consciousness with the word.[69] But one difference that must be acknowledged immediately is that, although Derrida deconstructs all books, all scriptures, privileging none, Bhartṛhari explicitly states that the Veda is the means for the realization of Brahman.[70]

Bhartṛhari is not simply privileging one book or one scripture over all others. His thought is more complex and subtle than that. On the one hand, as we have seen earlier, Bhartṛhari has said that the Veda is the *anukāra* of the *Śabdatattva;* that is, the Veda is the normative form of the manifested *Śabdatattva.* All other language is merely a further elaboration of the criterion manifestation of the *Śabdatattva* as the Veda. The Veda is not one book among others, it is the true manifestation of the *Śabdatattva.* This is why Bhartṛhari describes it in *Vākyapadīya* I:5 as both the *anukāra* and the *prāptyupāya* or means of realization of Brahman. On the other hand, however, Bhartṛhari also describes the science of grammar as the royal path and door to spiritual realization.[71] Grammar is no longer merely an aid to the study of the Veda but is itself a yoga or means to realization. This shift is possible because Bhartṛhari sees Veda as the manifestation of the *Śabdatattva* itself, grammar, as the science of the Veda, is at the same time the science of the *Śabdatattva* or Word-Principle itself and thus a yoga. A few verses later Bhartṛhari specifically describes a "Yoga preceded by the knowledge and use of the correct forms of words"; namely, the science of Grammar.[72] Later on in *Vākyapadīya* I:131, Bhartṛhari gives more detailed indications as to what this yoga of the word involves. I have given a detailed analysis of this passage elsewhere and will not repeat it here.[73] For our present purpose the important point to note is Bhartṛhari's focus on the individual's inner experience of language as involving an inner transformation—which parallels Derrida's emphasis on Grammatology as the science of writing before speech and in speech with power to change the individual's self-awareness.[74]

Bhartṛhari's emphasis on language as an inner transformative experience not only provides promising links with the modern thought of Derrida, but can also be seen as a compromise between the more individualistic Buddhists and Naiyāyikas. Carpenter puts it this way:

> This is the case because for Bhartṛhari, the Word-Principle is the foundation not only of the Veda

and the orthodox traditional world derived from it, but also of the individual's experience in appropriating that world. This experience is characterized by elements of genuine interiority, yet these elements are grounded in the same Word-Principle which manifests itself as the Veda.[75]

Like Derrida, however, Bhartṛhari analyzes the individual's inner experience not as the static presence of a set of divine words or forms (the *logos* model), nor as a superimposition of epistemological forms (Śaṅkara's *māyā*), but as an inner word that is primarily productive of activity and only secondarily productive of knowledge.[76] Bhartṛhari's *Śabdatattva,* the Word-Principle, is primarily an ontological principle and only secondarily epistemological.

We have seen how for Derrida the movement of language was a continuous sequencing of the arche-writing or trace into the spoken and written words, only to be thrown back again in a continual deconstructive reverse. The same kind of implosion-explosion cycle can be found in Bhartṛhari. Just as the *Śabdatattva* manifests itself objectively as the cosmos,[77] so the same Word-Principle manifests itself within each individual in his or her experience of language.[78] Within the individual the experience of the sequenced parts (letters and words) is subordinate to the unified whole (the sentence). Understanding of the sentence is possible only because its words taken together evoke a flash of illumination (*pratibhā* or *sphoṭa*) that is in some sense already prefigured (Derrida's arche-trace?) within consciousness.[79] This is due to the activity of the *Śabdatattva*. Bhartṛhari describes it as follows:

> When the meanings (of the individual words) have been understood separately, a flash of understanding takes place which they call the meaning of the sentence, brought about by the meanings of the individual words.
>
> It cannot be explained to others as such and such. It is experienced by everyone within himself and even the subject (of the experience) is not able to render an account of it to himself.
>
> It is something indefinable (avicāritā) and it brings about a kind of amalgamation of the meanings of individual words, covering the whole sentence as it were, it becomes its object.
>
> No one can avoid in one's activity that (flash of understanding) produced either through words or through the working of one's predispositions.[80]

This *pratibhā* or flash of understanding is insight into the whole meaning and form of the *Śabdatattva. Pratibhā* precedes and predisposes all human and animal activity. But it is also the culmination of our sequenced language activity as the illumination of the sentence. As such *pratibhā* is the means for the realization of the *Śabdatattva,* for they are but two sides of the same coin. *Pratibhā* is of the nature of one's inner self (*Śabdatattva*), but requires the words of language for its manifestation and realization.[81] Bhartṛhari's theory of intuition is not separate from his theory of language, but, indeed, is its fulfillment. *Pratibhā* is the experience in which the twofold manifestation of the *Śabdatattva* —as language and world, as knower and known— meet. This intuition is neither a purely subjective event nor an intuition of a thing-in-itself. "It is rather the intrinsic luminosity of the world as a dynamic interrelated whole which is revealed by language."[82] Language is the enactment of the interrelatedness of the manifested *Śabdatattva*. As Bhartṛhari puts it in *Vākyapadīya* III:2:14: "That one Reality is seen as the word, the meaning and their relation. It is the seen, the seeing, the see-er and the fruit of the seeing."[83] *Pratibhā* is the intuition of all of this and is described by Bhartṛhari as the light that removes ignorance. It is indefinable (*avicaritā*) because what it reveals is not some "thing," "idea," or "presence," but rather the dynamic interrelatedness of all things—an insight giving rise to action resulting in spiritual realization.

For both Derrida and Bhartṛhari, the science of Grammar enables one to experience language as more than purely epistemological in function. As we speak and write it, it "speaks and writes" us impelling us to action (*dharma*). Although it is clear that Bhartṛhari's speaking, writing, and acting of the word is a yoga or means of spiritual realization, Derrida offers only hints in that direction. It is clear that for Derrida the "theological" is a secondary manifestation of the trace, and that its problem and the problem with most Western metaphysics (and religion) is that the theological is a reification resulting from the surpressing of the *différance* inherent in language—the locus of its power in both spiritual and worldly action. Derrida's rejection of theology, metaphysics, and much philosophy is rooted in Bhartṛhari's observation that the dynamic interrelatedness of language cannot be described by the agent who experiences it. For both Bhartṛhari and Derrida any such description would be a reduction of the "dynamic interrelatedness of all experience" to some "thing" or "idea." Such a reductionism robs language of its power of action. This loss is simultaneously a loss of linguistic power and a loss of the power of spiritual realization.

For both Derrida and Bhartṛhari the correct understanding and practice of language results in a teleological transformation of experience. This common conclusion arises from remarkably different religious roots: Derrida from a prophetic critique of the Jewish and Christian experience of God; Bhartṛhari from an interpretation of Vedic *dharma* that took into account the Nyāya and Buddhist claims for individual spiritual experience.

We cannot say much of Derrida's religious roots and goal. In his relentless deconstruction of every logocentric theology, and even every negative theology, he keeps his spiritual self well hidden.[84] But perhaps this is the clue. Could it be that his spiritual source and vision is rooted in the Hebrew prophets? Just as Hebrew prophecy ruthlessly criticized every objectification of God, which packaged and separated God from the divine demand for ethical action in daily life,[85] so Derrida rigorously deconstructs all theology, philosophy, and ordinary language that objectifies our experience into false Gods and unreal presences. That Derrida's deconstruction does have a prophetic goal in suggested by his essay: "Of An Apocalyptic Tone Recently Adopted in Philosophy."[86] In this reading of the New Testament "Revelation or Apocalypse to John," Derrida suggests that the apocalyptic be considered "a transcendental condition of all discourse, of all experience itself, of every mark or every trace."[87] The Apocalypse of John, he suggests, could be taken as an exemplary revelation of this transcendental structure. And the theme of the Johannine Apocalypse he identifies as the recurrent and imperative "Come" of the text (Revelation 22:17–20). "Come" evokes both the imminent coming of the Lord and the imperative that the hearer come quickly. The call beyond being or *logos* itself comes from beyond being. It cannot come from a voice that is given any personification in our hearing of it—for that would be to "package" it in categories of presence. *Come* is plural in itself, in oneself. Its only content, says Derrida, is its resounding imperative tone[88] that calls forth action from us. The other characteristic of this exemplary book of Apocalypse is indicated in its final words "Do not seal [close] the words of the inspiration of this book." To seal is to encapsulate or close off the inherent "come" of language and/or as religion. The "Come" from beyond being and the imperative "Come" within oneself never close. The action of coming to the call that never ceases is the end to be realized. All of this fits well with the prophetic impulse of the Hebrew Bible. Its relentless negation of any conceptualization or speaking of the divine (the sin of idolatry), its prophetic hearing of the call to obedience that must always translate into action and its open-ended future that calls us to become to an end that is always simultaneously a new beginning—all of this seems to justify our rooting of Derrida in the spiritual critique of the Hebrew prophets, which Derrida has reformulated as a critique of all idolatrous use of language.

Like Derrida, Bhartṛhari's science of grammar is also a call to action, to *dharma*. Bhartṛhari reinterprets Vedic *dharma* as the *dharma* of the Word-

Principle, the *Śabdatattva*. This shift means that the *dharma* that one seeks to realize is no longer outside oneself, one's language, or the Veda, but is the very essence of one's consciousness. Just as for Derrida the voice of the prophetic "Come" becomes the "Come let us go," the inner voice of language, so also for Bhartṛhari, the Vedic *dharma* as the *Śabdatattva* becomes the *dharma* of "correct" language within individual consciousness. The purification of speech, the task of the traditional Vedic discipline of grammar, becomes the means for inner spiritualization.

Conclusion

This initial comparative study of Derrida's deconstructive Grammatology and Bhartṛhari's philosophy has proved stimulating and fruitful. It has identified many points of formal and often substantive contact between Derrida and traditional Indian thought. Further analysis of these areas of contact should prove challenging and invigorating for both Eastern and Western thought. That this will be the case has been exemplified in the specific comparison offered between Derrida and Bhartṛhari. This comparison has demonstrated new insights on both sides. Reading Bhartṛhari with Derrida highlights the error of previous interpretations that have read the *Vākyapadiyā* through decidedly Advaitic eyes. It has also highlighted the remarkable and original way in which Bhartṛhari accommodated the Buddhist and Nyāya stress on individual spiritual experience while yet retaining an orthodox grounding in Vedic *dharma,* now reinterpreted as *Śabdatattva.* Derrida's challenge to

Bhartṛhari would take the form of a throughgoing deconstruction of the *Vākyapadīya*. The most evident point of challenge here would be directed at Bhartṛhari's *Pratibhā* doctrine as a case of "mystical perception." This is, of course, the very criticism mounted against Bhartṛhari by the Mīmāṃsakas. As Derrida does not believe that anything like "pure" perception—perception free of representation or interpretation—exists,[89] his challenge is a significant one.

From the side of Western thought, the comparison has also been fruitful. It has called into question current suggestions that Derrida can be understood as a Mādhyamikan Buddhist—for this analysis shows him to agree with Bhartṛhari on exactly those points which separate Bhartṛhari and Nāgārjuna. The comparison with Bhartṛhari also suggests that Derrida's relation to scripture (as evidenced in his reading of Revelation) may well turn out to be functionally parallel to Bhartṛhari's handling of the Veda. Scripture is incorporated into the very structure of language and consciousness, thus becoming an ontological ground rather than a metaphysical object.

But perhaps even more important than what each side can learn about itself from the other are the significant points of common emphasis: that language is beginningless and coextensive with consciousness; that language is grounded in its dynamic sequencing by time rather than in any fixed structural forms; that this sequencing takes the form of the dynamic interrelatedness of the cosmos and carries within it an imperative call for action, that this call is obstructed or surpressed by our egocentric creation of concepts with which we identify ourselves as true presence (the sin of idolatry or the ignorance of *avidyā*); that the way to counteract this obstruction is the scientific deconstructing (Grammatology) or purifying (*Vyakāraṇa*) of language, which results in some form of "spiritual realization."

For the practice of philosophy, both Derrida and Bhartṛhari would reserve a high place. The task of philosophy is to deconstruct (Grammatology) or purify by linguistic criticism (*Vyakāraṇa*) language use in all the sciences. The specific application of this philosophic critique to religion was stated by Professor Murti in a way that Derrida and Bhartṛhari would perhaps both accept: "Without philosophical appraisal and critical alertness, religion would be blind, like the proverbial cock which had picked up a diamond but did not know its worth. It would degenerate into Dogma and Fanaticism."[90] The call of Derrida and Bhartṛhari is that philosophy (both Western and Indian) urgently needs to get on with its deconstructive and purifying task.

CHAPTER FOUR

DERRIDA AND ŚAṄKARA

THE preceding analysis of Bhartṛhari's Grammarian philosophy in relation to Derrida paves the way for a comparison of Derrida with Śaṅkara, probably India's best-known philosopher. Whereas our study of Bhartṛhari and Derrida turned up many points of similarity, our comparison of Derrida and Śaṅkara will reveal areas of sharp contrast. But before moving to our comparative study let us briefly situate Śaṅkara in the context of the Vedānta school of Indian philosophy.

The term *Vedānta* refers not only to a philosophical school but also to the Upaniṣads as the final sections of the Veda. Vedānta philosophy is the philosophy that gives further clarification to the insights offered in the Upaniṣads. It is thus a philosophy that sees itself as nothing more than a clear presentation of the Vedic teachings crystallized in the Upaniṣadic dialogues. However because these dialogues are often ambiguous there came to be several Vedānta philosophies corresponding to the differing interpretations of key Upaniṣadic texts, such as the great Upaniṣadic sentences or

Mahāvākyas. Thus interpretation (*mīmāṃsa*) is the basic activity of Vedānta philosophers. And they would agree with the modern thinker Hans-Georg Gadamer when he says "one understands *differently when one understands at all.*"[1] Interpretation is not a reproductive procedure by which a fixed cognitive meaning is extracted from the text. Rather, it is the production of an understanding that arises from the excess of meaning found in the text—an "excess" because it can never be encapsulated in words in such a way that all of its meaning is exhausted. Gadamer's view that the meaning of the text both elicits and includes in itself the varying interpretations through which it is transmitted[2] would square with the analysis of India's Vedānta scholars. But it was also their belief that the interpretation developed by their particular school most clearly exegeted the revealed truth of the scriptural sentences of the Upaniṣads.

Among the various Vedānta scholars who founded schools of philosophy, Śaṅkara is the most widely known. Scholars now place Śaṅkara at the end of the seventh century C.E.,[3] about two centuries after Bhartṛhari. Śaṅkara's school is referred to as Advaita or nondual Vedānta. It is clear that Śaṅkara knew Bhartṛhari's thought since he rejects Bhartṛhari's *Sphoṭa* theory of language. Śaṅkara's philosophy, and Vedānta in particular, is influenced by the Mīmāṃsa school of Indian philosophy—its view of language and the principles of interpretation. It would be fair to say that for Śaṅkara and his Advaita Vedānta school the overwhelming focus of attention was on interpreting the true meaning of Vedic scriptures—especially the role scripture plays in realizing *mokṣa* or liberation.[4] Derrida's philosophy also centers itself on theoretical insights relating to the interpretation of texts. It would be true to say that for both Derrida and Śaṅkara philosophy is to be understood as philosophy of language. And the focus of philosophy for both is on the way in which the interpretative function of language is to be understood in relation to the real.

This chapter will proceed by comparing Śaṅkara and Derrida on three points: the relation of language to the real; Śaṅkara versus Derrida on the nature of the real; and the end goal—language as a revelation of intuitive knowledge versus language as a call for action.

The Relation of Language to the Real

Derrida has attracted wide attention with his oft quoted phrase "Il n'y a pas de hors-texte" ("There is nothing outside of the text"). Philosophers who see language as functioning by symbolizing an external referent (e.g., the view that the word *God* has for its referent a real divinity that exists over and above the word) find Derrida's statement to be both outrageous and wrong. Derrida's denial of "a real" existing outside of the text is seen to be a denial of reality, a denial of God, and at best, some new form of nihilism. Śaṅkara would also disagree with Derrida. For Śaṅkara there is a real that exists over and above language; namely, Brahman.

In the previous chapters we found that Derrida often comes close to the Grammarian perspective of Bhartṛhari and his view that language and consciousness are beginninglessly identified with each other. Yet when we place Śaṅkara's thought in close proximity with the thought of Derrida, new aspects of Derrida are highlighted. Just as for Śaṅkara the real, Brahman, is fully seen only when language is negated, so also Derrida, in discussing "Edmond Jabès and the Question of the Book" comments that for Judaism God is not known directly through the Book but when we keep still.[5] Then God comes to us in action, questioning us, demanding a moral response. Unlike the perfect stillness of the Greek *logos* or Śaṅkara's Brahman (which is perfect being and bliss[6]), Derrida following Jabès talks of a God who constantly questions out of silence. This questioning comes from a rupture within God as the origin of history. Derrida quotes Reb Lema, "Do not forget that you are the nucleus of a rupture" and goes on to say:

> God separated himself from himself in order to let us speak, in order to astonish and to interrogate us. He did so not by speaking but by keeping still, by letting silence interrupt his voice and his signs, by letting the Tables be broken. In *Exodus* God repented . . . between original speech and writing and, within Scripture, between the origin and the repetition (*Exodus* 32:14; 33:17). Writing is, thus, originally hemeretic and secondary. Our writing, certainly, but already His, which starts with the stifling of his voice and the dissimulation of his Face. This difference, this negativity in God is our freedom, the transcendence and the verb which can relocate the purity of their negative origin only in the possibility of the Question.[7]

There is a dynamism, an originary force here that is not found in the Greek *logos* nor in Śaṅkara's Brahman. It is a reality that starts with

God's silent desire to speak. Out of that silence comes not only His speech and ours but also, because of the questioning silence, our freedom to act. But with this freedom comes the responsibility interrogated in God's written and silent questioning. But to be heard, language, both His and ours, must be silenced.

Śaṅkara would agree with Jabès and Derrida that our language and even the revealed language of the Veda ultimately must be silenced for the real, Brahman, to be "seen." This is indeed the goal of Śaṅkara's disciplined meditation—to hear (*śravaṇa*), think (*manana*), and reflect (*nididhāsana*).[8] But Śaṅkara takes pains to make clear that hearing, thinking, and reflecting are not activities nor are they to be understood as injunctions from Scripture. Śaṅkara's concern here is to separate the realization of Brahman from any motivated action, since in his system such action is necessarily tainted with egoism's desire for a result—which itself will obstruct the real. For Śaṅkara, Brahman, the real, exists separate from language and action and reveals itself only when language, its actions and questionings are cancelled out—as in the final direct perception prompted by meditation on *Tat tvam asi* ("That thou art")—so that Brahman alone remains.[9] But Brahman is experienced as pure being and pure bliss rather than the kind of freedom-giving but everdisturbing questioner of Jabès and Derrida.

For Śaṅkara language is a part of *māyā* (our worldly experience) and is ultimately unreal for it disappears when Brahman, the real, is "seen." But this does not mean that language is not to be valued.

Indeed, for Śaṅkara, language as Veda is the only means by which Brahman, the real, can be realized.

But even the best language, the *mahāvākyas* of the Upaniṣads, must be left behind for the *anubhava* or direct experience of Brahman to occur. This is clearly evidenced by Śaṅkara's theory of error in which the realization of Brahman is simultaneous with the cancellation of the *mahāvākya*—or, to evoke the favorite Vedāntin analogy, the snake disappears completely when the rope is seen. Ultimately, then for Śaṅkara, it is the Upaniṣadic *neti neti* (not this, not that), speech as a *via negativa* to the real, that characterizes Śaṅkara's theory of language in relation to the real.

By contrast, even though he too stresses the need for silence Derrida never ends up in a silence totally transcendent of language. Derrida, in his reading of Jabès describes God's silence as that which both speaks and stifles itself so that we may have freedom to hear and be heard. Meanings and questions for us "ooze out" from around the letters and spoken sounds to emerge not in propositions but in silences—blanks.[10] Language, even the language of the Book, ends in silence, (both agree on this), but a silence filled with the tension of divine interrogation rather than Śaṅkara's pure bliss.

Śaṅkara versus Derrida on the Nature of the Real

As we have seen, for Śaṅkara language, even the language of the Veda, has to be cancelled out or transcended for the real to be experienced. This is because the essential characteristic of language is difference, and difference is antithetical to identity, which characterizes the monism of Śaṅkara's Advaita theory.[11] As an Advaitin, Śaṅkara maintains, from various identity statements in the

Upaniṣads, that all difference is negated and transcended in the direct experience of the real. Śaṅkara emphasizes the impossibility of using the diversity of language, even the higher language of the *jñānakāṇḍa* (Vedic passages relating to knowledge), directly to designate reality.[12] For Śaṅkara, the recognition of distinctions between things is of the nature of *avidyā* or ignorance and is that which obstructs the recognition of the real. Language, due to its necessary conceptualization of reality into words and sentences, becomes a part of that difference that obscures the real. The difference of all language is part of the *māyā* that hides Brahman from our view.

Whereas difference is the *avidyā* to be overcome for Śaṅkara, difference as manifested in the dynamic tension of language is the real for Derrida. All language, says Derrida, finds its source in "difference" (as the linguist Saussure had claimed).[13] In Derrida's view it is precisely this general movement of difference that is the arche-trace that contains within it the possibility for all speech and writing. The real is nothing but the dynamic expressive difference of language. It is this moment of difference that permits all thought, speech, and writing and makes possible the opposition between signifier and signified.[14] The functional parallel for *avidyā* (Śaṅkara's notion of the obstruction of the real) is, for Derrida, the privileging of one of the opposites of language over the other, and thereby destroying the dynamic tension between the opposites. The tension between the opposites is, for Derrida, the hallmark of the real. This is the hidden intent behind the term *deconstruction* when used in connection with Derrida's thought. What is being deconstructed by

Derrida, in his analysis of language use, is the human privileging of one of the pairs of opposites over the other. This privileging of good over evil, identity over difference, and man over woman has typified Western thought. The second term of these pairs is always seen as a corrupted version of the first. Evil is seen as the lack of good, and difference as an obstruction of identity.[15] The opposites are not maintained in dynamic tension, but are placed in a hierarchical order that gives the first priority. As a result much philosophy has engaged in a privileging of identity over difference.

At this point Derrida would apparently be offering a critique of Śaṅkara's emphasis on identity. However, on closer analysis the two are seen to be engaged in a similar philosophical tactic. Just as Śaṅkara would use the conceptual term *identity* as simply a hint or pointer to the nature of the real, so also Derrida admits that his use of *difference* to indicate the nature of the real must be constantly deconstructed. Both Śaṅkara and Derrida agree that the conceptual oppositions that make up language are the obstacles that get in our way of the experience of the real. Identifying oneself with either of the terms that make up these oppositions (e.g., *identity* for Śaṅkara; *difference* for Derrida) is the trap of language that must be overcome. For Śaṅkara the only way out is to transcend language altogether, so that all of the opposites and indeed all conceptualizing is cancelled by the direct intuition (*anubhava*) of the real. By contrast, Derrida thinks this trap may be escaped by staying within language but on the middle path between the pairs of opposites. When the opposites of language are maintained in dynamic tension, through a continual deconstruction of first one opposite and then the other, the real is experienced. For the moment the real is spoken it is tending to swing the pendulum of language toward either one or the other of the opposites. Only by a continual deconstructing and reversing of each pendulum swing may we experience the real as the middle point—where the tension between the pairs is momentarily in balance. For Derrida, the constant change and challenge that this deconstruction requires is not a cause for lament—it is rather the recognition that such a process, with its ongoing need for deconstruction, is itself the real. Again we are reminded of Mādhyamika and the relentless critique of the *catuṣkoṭi* as the basic task of philosophy. Derrida would agree, but he would deny the Buddhist and Advaita contention that another option is open; namely, the transcending of the trap of language altogether. For Derrida there is no *anubhava* or *śūnya* experience of the real outside of language. At this point Derrida is a typical Westerner in his view that it is in the midst of the existential struggle, not beyond it, that the real is most fully realized.

Derrida's position is clearly revealed in his critical reading of Rousseau. In spite of his attempt to maintain an original "natural" order of values for humanity, language, and society, Rousseau is forced, as Derrida demonstrates, to admit that there is never a moment of pure being or presence—as the Western logocentric tradition and Śaṅkara attempt to maintain. Always at the source Derrida is able to find a moment of *differance,* a rupture of the divine, a falling away from nature, the origins of speech or even the experience of pure melody in music without the implicit presence of harmony.[16] Thus the impossibility of the everpresent desire to experience the real as pure presence.[17] Śaṅkara would agree with Derrida that so long as one stays in the lower realms of language and music the bliss of pure presence, so desired by Rousseau, is an impossibility. But although Derrida stops with the revelation of the divine rupture and the impossible possibility that results from the experience of the real as difference, Śaṅkara goes on to a *nirguṇa* or qualityless level of experience where the existential frustrations of difference that characterize *māyā* or this world are totally transcended. One gets completely out of all the obstructions of language, with the help of language—the revealed words of the Veda—to the pure presence of Brahman (being, consciousness, and bliss). In Śaṅkara's view Derrida's description of the real is quite correct for the lower level of reality, the level of *māyā*. Derrida's failure in Śaṅkara's view, is his unwillingness to study the special words of the Veda with such seriousness and intensity that he is "pole-vaulted" right out of the realm of language and difference into the direct *anubhava* or self-realization of Brahman. Even when Derrida discusses the silence of God in his reading of "Edward Jabès and the Question of the Book" he remains in the realm of a divine questioning that betrays the lower (*saguṇa*) level of knowledge of Brahman. For his part Derrida would maintain that Śaṅkara's so-called lower or *saguṇa* level exhausts our experience of the real. To think of a higher level of pure identity or pure Brahman is foolishly to attempt to escape the dynamic existential tension and demands of difference to be found in the barest melody or even in the silent questioning of God that squeezes itself between the letters and words of scripture.

THE END GOAL: LANGUAGE AS A REVELATION OF KNOWLEDGE (ŚAṄKARA) VERSUS LANGUAGE AS A CALL FOR ACTION (DERRIDA)

Both Śaṅkara and Derrida have a practical goal in mind in their philosophy of language. For them, the philosophy of language is not just abstract theorizing; it has the practical goal of spiritual self-realization. Between them, however, the nature of this self-realization is quite different: for Śaṅkara it requires the total transcending of language, whereas for Derrida it is found in the prophetic call for action that comes to us from the very midst of language itself.

As noted at the outset, Śaṅkara's Advaita is essentially a philosophy of exegesis—a way of coming to the true meaning of scripture. Śaṅkara's approach is to divide the Vedic corpus that includes the *saṃhitā* (poetic hymns), *brāhmaṇa* (directions for sacrifice), and *upaniṣads* into two categories: a lower one dealing with actions (*karmakāṇḍa*), a higher one dealing with knowledge (*jñānakāṇḍa*).[18] The Pūrva Mīmāṃsa philosophy of language, with its emphasis upon the verb as conveying the meaning of the sentence (i.e., an injunction to action) is taken by Śaṅkara as an appropriate form of exegesis for the *karmakāṇḍa* texts. But this Pūrva Mīmāṃsa approach is not applicable to the *jñānakāṇḍa* texts of the Upaniṣads that tell us of the identity of the Self with Brahman. Statements such as *"Tat tvam asi"* are not injunctions but declarations of fact "statements whose subject matter exists already, that is Brahman, or the Self."[19] Whereas in the first approach people see themselves as agents following scriptural injunctions and engaging in religious rituals to achieve results (e.g., rebirth in heaven or *svarga*), the *jñānakāṇḍa,* by contrast, is seen by Śaṅkara as addressing a separate group of people —those who have become eligible to hear the statements about Brahman by virtue of their moral purity, intelligence, and intense spiritual desire for release. Because the whole point of statements like the *mahāvākyas* or the *neti, neti* sentences is to imply that there are no differences in the real, they can be comprehended only by someone who is just on the verge of the *anubhava* experience—the direct realization that the real, Brahman, the Self is without distinctions.[20] We will have to come back to the question of just how Śaṅkara understands that the sentences of the *jñānakāṇḍa* are able to produce this result, but first let us look at Derrida's approach to self-realization.

Although Derrida deconstructs the metaphysics of *logos,* presence, or any suggestion of theistic religion, there is a teleology that may be found in his philosophy of language. In *Of Grammatology* Derrida discusses the nature of the arche-trace. This trace, like the *Śabdatattva* of Bhartṛhari, contains within itself all the possibilities of manifestation as the primordial "difference." This "difference" is the inherent teleological force within us that leads to self-manifestation.[21] And this self-manifestation is structured according to the diverse possibilities of the trace. The general characteristic of the manifested trace is that of temporal becoming. Within this becoming, the theological is but one moment in the total movement of the trace.[22] The trace with its seed of difference, is not more biological than spiritual, but in its manifestation is found the possibility for all the pairs of opposites. The existential experience of this dynamic process of becoming is for Derrida the realization of the spiritual whole. Such a realization is achieved by the deconstruction of the illusions of permanence, stasis, or presence that are constantly being superimposed on the becoming of language. To understand this whole process of becoming of language is itself the spiritual whole.

As we saw in Chapter 3, this deconstructive process is not seen by Derrida as abstract theorizing. Rather, we are deconstructing our very selves in this process. The language we are deconstructing is our own thinking and speaking—our own consciousness. Deconstruction is thus the existential process of becoming self-aware, of self-realization. As we think, speak, and write, language speaks and writes us, impelling us into action. As was previously suggested in Chapter 3, the spiritual sources of this call for action seem to be rooted in the Hebrew prophetic tradition with its call for action and its ruthless criticism of every objectification that packaged and separated God from the divine demand for ethical action in daily life.[23] So also Derrida rigorously deconstructs all theology, philosophy, and ordinary language that objectifies our experience into false gods and unreal presences and, in so doing, removes us from the imperative of God's call to moral action.[24]

One of the places in Derrida's writing where this emphasis on moral action is most clearly seen is in his brilliant essay "Violence and Metaphysics: An Essay on the Thought of Emmanuel Levinas."[25] In

Levinas Derrida finds a clear analysis of the epistemological emphasis of the Greek tradition of metaphysics (which has largely determined Western philosophy) and its violent encounter with an alien mode of thought—the ethical thrust of Hebrew thought.[26] Levinas presents us with a summons to move from the Greek metaphysics of presence, which seeks to absorb all differences into identity, toward prophetic speech with its strong ethical impulse. For Levinas the ethical relationship is "the only one capable of opening the space of transcendence and of liberating metaphysics."[27] Rather than ethics being seen as a second-order consideration arising from and founded on epistemology (the dominant view of Western philosophy), Levinas proposes an ethics that would not be subject to the governing interests of epistemology but be grounded in a recourse to experience as understood within the context of Hebrew messianic eschatology.[28] Within this analysis of experience the Other, and our ethical relationship with the Other, is the imperative.

In Derrida's essay Levinas explores the limits of the Greek tradition by placing it in dialogue with the ethical imperative of the Hebrew tradition. Rather than a metaphysics of *logos* and light, Levinas finds himself led by the Hebrew paradigm of relationship with the Other to a kind of discourse that can be grasped only between the self and the human other.[29] It is this human encounter that is fundamental, and not the Greek method of knowing by the relationship between the mind and its object, which produces ethics only as a secondary consideration. As with Martin Buber, the I-Thou relationship is primary for philosophy.[30] All philosophy must take its rise from the face-to-face context. The foundation of metaphysics for Levinas is found in the resemblance between humans and God, between the human visage and the face of the divine. For us, the Other in our relationships resembles God. Thus human discourse is properly understood only if it is seen as discourse with God. Such discourse presupposes separation rather than identity with God.[31]

For Levinas, and I think for Derrida, all of this is grounded in God who appears to us as difference, as other, as a Thou in relation with our own I.[32] Without this difference, this God who breaches space, there would be no time or history for the unbroken identity of the Greeks would be the sole existent. God as the infinitely Other, creates the context for all relationship that is also the context for all language.[33] And the fundamental philosophical content of this language of human relationship is a call for ethical action. But Derrida pushes Levinas's thought even further. The separation required for discourse with God means that we are created in his image not "in terms of communion or knowledge, nor in terms of participation and incarnation. . . . [Rather] we are 'in the Trace of God'."[34] This trace shows itself not in presence but in the absence of God.

> The Face of God disappears forever in showing itself. . . . The face of Yahweh is the *total* person and the *total* presence of "the Eternal speaking face to face with Moses," but saying to him also: "Thou canst not see my face: for there shall be no man see me and live . . . thou shalt stand upon a rock and it shall come to pass, while my glory passeth by, that I will put thee in a cleft of the rock, and

> will cover thee with my hand while I pass by: And I will take away mine hand, and thou shalt see my back parts: but my face shall not be seen (Exodus 33:20-23). The face of God which commands while hiding itself is at once more and less a face than all faces.[35]

Derrida goes on to suggest that Levinas is perhaps coming very close to Jabès when he says "All faces are His; this is why HE has no face?"[36] It is in our relationship with other faces that we encounter the God who is otherwise absent to us.

In many ways this approach of Derrida's is just the opposite of that of Śaṅkara. For Śaṅkara language is primarily epistemological in function. For him self-realization is not the realization that we ourselves are the text (Derrida's position), but rather the realization that language is the *māyā* that is totally transcended when the real, Brahman, is seen. For Śaṅkara the goal is not to be impelled into action by language (Derrida's view) but to transcend language and action and realize the direct knowledge of Brahman.

In a very real sense Śaṅkara's view of language is ambivalent. Because language is the instrument of *avidyā* breeding mental constructions that distort reality by hiding our true Self from us, Śaṅkara is suspicious of language. On the other hand, he recognizes that without language, especially the speech of the *jñānakāṇda, mokṣa* cannot be realized. Although the great sentences of the Upaniṣads are ultimately fake (because they are language and as such the products of *avidyā*) still, says Śaṅkara, one can be liberated by hearing a falsehood, just as one can be killed by being frightened by an illusory snake. Śaṅkara's theory of language, like his theory of error, is that the erroneous, in this case the scriptural sentence, must be completely cancelled for the real to be known. The two are mutually exclusive. This is clearly very different from Derrida, where the real is seen to be in the very midst of the tension between the pairs of opposites of language. To transcend this tension, to get out of language altogether, is, for Derrida, an impossibility whereas, for Śaṅkara, it is both possible and necessary.

But how does Śaṅkara suggest that one can get out of language? It requires that one learn another way of hearing the word, a way in which words no longer function as a direct designation of reality. The correct hearing of *mahāvākya* gives no positive description of Brahman. For the properly prepared mind it is simply the occasion for the realization that knowledge of Brahman is not conceptual at all, but rather a direct intuition (*anubhava*) that is free from the taint of words or any of the other ordinary means of knowing.[37] Whereas Derrida's discriminative deconstruction constantly goes on as the very essence of reality, for Śaṅkara, after the *anubhava* or direct intuition of Brahman, no reflective consideration is possible for there is no language or thought content left to reflect upon. Whereas for Derrida there is nothing outside of language or the text, for Śaṅkara there is nothing of the text left in the *anubhava* experience. The text is the subject that the Upaniṣadic *"neti, neti"* cancels out to enable the real to be known.

For both Śaṅkara and Derrida the goal of spiritual self-realization depends on the correct understanding of language and results in a transformation of our ordinary way of knowing. However, this common conclusion arises from remarkably different religious roots: Derrida from a critique of the Jewish and Christian understanding of God; Śaṅkara from an interpretation of the Veda.

CONCLUSION

This initial comparative study of Derrida and Śaṅkara on language has proven stimulating and fruitful. It has identified points of formal and at times substantive contact between Derrida and traditional Indian philosophy.

In terms of the nature of the real, Derrida and Śaṅkara clearly find themselves in opposite camps. Whereas difference is the *avidyā* to be overcome for Śaṅkara, difference manifested in the dynamic tension of language is the real for Derrida. This distinction, as we saw, carries over into their contrasting perceptions of the end-goal. For Derrida this difference manifests itself as a call for moral action. For Śaṅkara the action associated with difference is understood as the *saguṇa* Brahman that must be negated for the *nirguṇa* or qualityless Brahman to be experienced.

It is at precisely this point that Derrida would surely challenge Śaṅkara's notion of *anubhava* as a pure perception free of the *avidyā* of language. Because Derrida does not believe that anything like "pure perception"—that is, perception free of representation or interpretation—exists,[38] his challenge to Śaṅkara is a significant one.

Chapter Five

Derrida and Aurobindo

A trace *(Spur)* is left in our psychical apparatus of the perceptions which impinge upon it. This we may describe as a "memory trace" . . . [and] memory traces can only consist in permanent modifications of the elements of the system . . . [yet the same system must] remain perpetually open to the reception of fresh occasions for modification.

—Derrida quoting Freud's description of the requirements for the mystic writing-pad.[1]

In the glow of the Spirit's room of memories
He could recover the luminous marginal notes
Dotting with light the crabbed ambiguous scroll,
Rescue the preamble and the saving clause
Of the dark Agreement by which all is ruled
That rises from material Nature's sleep.
To clothe the Everlasting in new shapes.

—Aurobindo, *Savitri*[2]

In contrast with Śaṅkara's view of language as ultimately separate from Brahman, Aurobindo returns much closer to Bhartṛhari. For Aurobindo, the modern Indian poet and philosopher, language is the dynamic foundation out of which self-consciousness, culture, and religion arise. Each language is the self-expression and power of the soul of the people that naturally speaks it.[3] "Language is the sign of the cultural life of a people, the index of its soul in thought and mind that stands behind and enriches its soul in action."[4] Like Bhartṛhari and Derrida, Aurobindo conceives of language as having two senses: the inner intuited sense and the outer material manifestation as spoken words. Aurobindo's thinking would seem to parallel Bhartṛhari's analysis of *śabda* or speech into *artha* (inner sound) and *dhvani* (outer sound),[5] as well as Derrida's division of the linguistic sign into signified (inner abstract concept) and signifier (spoken and heard sound).[6] What makes Aurobindo's thought on language especially interesting is that he incorporates into his otherwise traditional Indian thought an evolutionary principle. This at once separates him from the classical ideas of Bhartṛhari and Śaṅkara, but, strangely, does not make him modern enough for Derrida. There are, however, some interesting points of similarity between Derrida and Aurobindo. These will be examined in three sections: the pure possibility of language; poetry and the cycles of language; and the need for deconstruction.

THE PURE POSSIBILITY OF LANGUAGE

Both Derrida and Aurobindo conceive of language as grounded in a state of pure possibility. For Derrida this is the a priori state of arche-writing or difference, the condition out of which all language arises.[7] For Aurobindo language is grounded in root sounds that contain the possibility for a multiplicity of signification to evolve.[8] Both see the need to keep language open to its pure possibility. Both offer analyses of how the present state of language has tended to close off the development of the originary possibility—the logocentricism of Western metaphysics for Derrida; the evolution of language into fixed forms in which the multisignificant possibility of root sounds is lost for Aurobindo. For both there is a need for deconstruction (Derrida) or reevolution (Aurobindo) so that the pure possibility of language may again function. Both have the problem of explaining how language can leave memory traces that are relatively permanent and yet, at the same time, remain perpetually open to the reception of fresh occasions for modification—like Freud's mystic writing-pad. Only if these two conditions are met is the pure possibility of language, which both Derrida and Aurobindo value, safeguarded.

In his essay "Force and Signification" Derrida comments on the restriction of possibility involved in speaking and writing: "the necessarily restricted passageway of speech against which all possible meanings push each other, preventing each other's emergence. Speaking frightens me because, by never saying enough, I also say too much. And if the necessity of becoming breath or speech restricts meaning—and our responsibility for it—writing restricts and constrains speech further still."[9] The absence of language is pregnant with the pure possibility of all language. But as soon as signification begins this infinite possibility is reduced and specified in ways that are ultimately problematic. It is the anguish of choice between the various possibilities, the anguish that makes it so hard to begin to speak or write. But once we begin we are committed to a particular pathway that is simultaneously a gain and a loss—a gain in specificity of conceptual meaning and a corresponding loss of possibility. Every writing or speaking is therefore inaugural, because of the absolute freedom of speech initially enjoyed.[10]

For Aurobindo such an inauguration of speech, with its corresponding loss of pure possibility, is thought of as occurring not every time we speak, as is the case with Derrida, but early in the history of the evolution of language. In "The Origins of Aryan Speech"[11] Aurobindo presents his theory of the origin and evolution of language most fully. Through a comparative study of Sanskrit, Latin, Greek, and Tamil he arrives at certain tentative conclusions. His method is to go back to the earliest forms and trace their development into modern speech. Whereas modern speech "is largely a fixed and almost artificial form, not precisely a fossil, but an organism proceeding towards fossilisation," earlier forms of language were fluid and multisignificant.[12] Aurobindo traces the evolutionary process found in Sanskrit (in his view the purest and most perfected language) as follows.[13] In Vedic times each mantric seed-sound was a focus of vibration not fixed to any precise idea. It had a general *guṇa* or quality that could evoke a number of possible significances. At first, therefore, word clans developed with a common stock of possible meanings and a communal right to call upon any of them. Individuality occurred in the shades of expression given to the same ideas rather than an exclusive right of a particular sound to any one idea. Language gradually evolved from this communal life of words to something specific and fixed. "The progression is from the general to the particular, from the vague to the precise, from the physical to the mental, from the concrete to the abstract, from the expression of an abundant variety of sensations about similar things to the expression of precise difference between similar things, feelings and actions."[14] In the first state the spoken word is more dominant than its idea—sound determines sense. Later on, the idea becomes all important—the sound secondary. This evolution of language takes place by the repeated association of ideas with specific *mantras* until the multisignificance of the original root sound is narrowed down by usage into a fixed relationship with a particular idea. Knowledge of the history of this evolution of language is essential for attempting interpretations or translations of texts, such as the Vedas, that come from an earlier period of more fluid linguistic function. By the use of tools such as Pāṇini's Grammar and Yaska's lexicon Aurobindo believes it is possible to work "backward," as it were, and recover the past history of individual words. One can then establish the meanings possessed by them at different stages of their evolution, and so restore to words their lost significances. In this way the clear possibilities of various meanings can be established for the actual text of a Vedic hymn. Aurobindo concludes: "The rest is a matter of comparative study of passages in which the word occurs and of constant fitness in the context. I have continually found that a sense thus restored illumines always the context whenever it is applied and on the other hand that a sense demanded always by the context is precisely that to which we are led by the history of the word."[15] The results of the application of this approach are available in Aurobindo's interpretation-translation of the Vedas, Upaniṣads, and the Gītā.[16]

But there are philosophical implications as well; namely, that by reversing the history of the evolution of language one can get back to the mystical inner sense that lies buried behind the fixed external meanings. Although Derrida would not agree with Aurobindo's privileging of original sounds, as this leads to a phonocentric philosophy of language, Derrida shares Aurobindo's view that the patterns of language established by usage need constant deconstructing to free up language to its multitude of possibility. Nor does Derrida see this as a problem mainly resulting from the historical evolution of language, as does Aurobindo. In Derrida's view every speaking or writing tends to privilege one possibility over others and thus must be deconstructed if language is to retain its fullest freedom.

Aurobindo, by contrast, focuses more on the historical development from the general to the particular, which he finds to be present in all languages. However, he suggests that this process is most clearly seen in Sanskrit. Because the Sanskrit dissolved early into the Prakrit languages, says Aurobindo, it did not reach the final stage typical of most modern languages, where the world has "shrunk" to a fixity in its concrete significance. Even in its most advanced literary forms Sanskrit retains a wealth of synonyms and an astounding capacity for rhetorical devices—especially for the double sense or *śleṣa*.[17] Vedic Sanskrit represents an earlier stratum abounding in a variety of forms and inflexions; it is fluid and yet richly subtle in its use of cases and tenses. "The word for the Vedic Rishi," says Aurobindo, "is still a living thing, a thing of power, creative, formative. It is not yet a conventional symbol for an idea, but itself the parent and former of ideas. It carries within it the memory of its roots, is still conscient of its own history."[18] The Vedic *mantra* is still vibrating in tune with what Aurobindo calls "a corresponding originative vibration on the supramental at the very root of things."[19] And what is it that is at the root of things? Brahman, says Aurobindo. But words even the words of the Vedas are not Brahman. Aurobindo sees Brahman as efficient but not material cause of language and scripture. Human speech is only a secondary expression of the transcendent Brahman. Even the vibrations of the Vedic *mantras,* though they serve to reveal Brahman to us, are only a far-off resonance of the perfectly vibrant supreme truth.[20]

Aurobindo took this Tantric resonance theory very literally—it formed the basis for his psychology of the word. For us today the English terms *wolf* or *cow* simply designate particular animals. We have no knowledge of those sounds as being especially fitting. By contrast, says Aurobindo, the Vedic Rishi experienced the mantric vibration *Vṛka* as the tearer, and *dhenu* as the fosterer or nourisher. These original general meanings are resonances of aspects of the Divine first and only secondarily are used to designate—among other things—a wolf and a cow. Such sound vibrations functioned very fluidly in the mind of the Vedic poet—sometimes referencing a merely conventional image but at other times losing sight of a specific image completely and evoking a general intuition, for example, the universe as fosterer or nourisher.[21] To take another example, Agni at the lowest level may have meant simply the god of the Vedic fire. But to those sensitive to its deeper psychological vibrations Agni evoked "the idea of the illumined Energy which builds up the worlds and which exalts man to the Highest, the doer of the great work, the Purohit of the human sacrifice."[22] In later ages, says Aurobindo, the intellect intervened with a demand for greater economy and precision resulting in a progressive loss of the bearing capacity of words. The word shrank into its outer concrete significance. The fluid evocative power of the inner word was largely lost. "The letter lived on when the spirit was forgotten; the symbol, the body of the doctrine, remained, but the soul of knowledge had fled from its coverings."[23] Aurobindo saw his own poetry and his translations of Veda, Upaniṣad, and Gītā as efforts at restoring to the word its double psychological sense—a spiritual inner evocation as well as an outer concrete reference—and a restoring to language a degree of its original freedom and possibility.[24]

Although Derrida would criticize Aurobindo's theory for privileging the sound over the letter, he would support Aurobindo's aim at keeping language as free and flexible as possible. For Derrida language loses this freedom when it becomes locked into a one-sided pattern of signification, as has happened in the logocentric tradition of Western metaphysics. Such closed patterns are seen by Derrida as totalitarian because they block the freedom of language and restrict it to a particular one-sided structure of meaning. Language thus has the potential to be a double-edged sword. On the one hand, it has the positive function of signifying and conveying meaning. On the other hand, once spoken or written it can function negatively to restrict or close off further signification. Derrida catches this double possibility in his reading of Plato's *Phaedrus* and Plato's use of the Greek word *pharmakon.*[25]

The two chief senses of *pharmakon* are "poison" and "cure." Derrida's reading of the *Phaedrus* demonstrates that throughout the text "writing" is both poison and cure. Whereas on the one hand writing is a threat to the living presence of authentic spoken language, on the other it is an indispensable means for anyone who wants to record, transmit, or somehow commemorate that presence.[26] Derrida goes on to show that all language has this *pharmakon* or double-sided possibility. This is why language use is described by Derrida as a fearful experience. It is a necessity for us if we are to communicate. Yet as soon as we begin to speak or write we loose the multiplicity and freedom present in the absence of speech. When we speak we are conscious of saying both too much *and* not enough.[27] What is worse, whatever we say can be structured into a closed system of meaning that is absolutistic and totalitarian in nature. Such one-sided closed systems have become the basis for a one-sided ethic, such as the privileging of males over females or speech over writing. One-sided signification of meaning is not just a problem for philosophy, it has a fundamental ethical impact on our human interrelationships. Thus, in Derrida's view, language use can be either poison or cure on many different levels of experience. Consequently, anguish is involved in the choices made in speaking—and we constantly need to criticize or deconstruct these choices to keep the potential for future language use fresh and open. Not surprisingly Derrida is critical of philosophies that claim to have comprehended the structure of truth, for implicit in such a claim is the reification of language, the closing off of its choices, and the loss of the sense of anguish. As Derrida enigmatically puts it, "it is to lose meaning by finding it."[28]

Although Derrida would certainly not be comfortable with Aurobindo's placing of the originary power of language in an a priori root sound, he would agree with Aurobindo that the goal is to keep language free from fixed formulations—especially as these rapidly become one-sided. Such situations not only result in a loss of the freedom, the pure possibility of language, but they also have ethical implications.

Poetry and the Cycles of Language

Poetry is special because of its ability to reach the pure possibility of language. In this sense it is often the initiator of cycles of language. In his essay on "Force and Signification" Derrida says that the revelatory power of poetry "is indeed the access to free speech."[29] This occurs, in Aurobindo's view, by virtue of the poet's sensitivity to the inner vibrations of the transcendent realm. If well fashioned the poet's words provide a means for crossing over from the spiritual to the concrete—for Aurobindo best exemplified in the *mantras* of the Vedas. These seed-sound *mantras* represent concentration points of transcendental energy from which evolutionary spiritual growth can take place.[30] Derrida, in his essay "Edmond Jabès and the Question of the Book," offers a similar formulation: "To be a poet is to know how to leave speech. To let it speak alone, which it can only do in its written form. *To leave* writing is to be there only in order to provide its passageway, to be the diaphanous element of its going forth: everything and nothing."[31] The poet by his or her absence allows language free access to its full range of possibility. The poet's absence is an absence of ego, of ego-determined language, that allows a total transparency to the word. As Derrida puts it in "Force and Signification," only *pure absence* can inspire—the absence of everything in which presence is announced.[32] In Aurobindo's thought *pure absence* is not just a theoretical formulation but a true description of the egoless state of the Vedic poets who were psychically transparent to the original *mantras*, the seed-words for all later language. It is unclear as to whether Derrida would see "pure absence" as the complete purging out of ego in the manner accepted by Aurobindo's Eastern thought. However both agree that the poet's *absence* (however understood) opens the way for the inspired, full, and free formulation of language. And in this event is its birth.

Two of Derrida's essays relate the experience of the poet to Jewish as opposed to Greek religious experience. In "Force and Signification" Derrida remarks that poetic writing is the anguish of *ruach*—Hebrew for God's Spirit, but also for wind and human breath or life force—experienced in solitude, a solitude that includes human ethical responsibility. This was the experience of the prophet Jeremiah, for example, hearing the *ruach* of God and writing or dictating it as poetry. "It is the moment at which we must *decide* whether we will engrave what we hear. And whether engraving preserves or betrays speech."[33] This experience of poets, prophets, and seers is *inaugural*. But it is also dangerous and anguishing because one does not know where it is going. Thus the reluctance of Jeremiah to speak God's words.[34] Yet this inaugural poetic writing embodies meaning. As Derrida puts it, "Meaning is neither before nor after the act. Is not that which is called God, that which imprints every human course and recourse with its secondarity, the passageway of deferred reciprocity between reading and writing? or the absolute witness to the dialogue in which what one sets out to write has already been read, and what one sets out to say is already a response, the third party as the transparency of meaning."[35]

In another essay "Edmond Jabès and the Question of the Book" Derrida also speaks of absence, poetic anguish, and Jewish experience. If God opens language and poetry by his inspiration, he is at the same time its absence and separation. Unlike the Greek *logos* idea where truth precedes and language simply represents it, the Jewish way of language "preceded by no truth . . . is the way through the Desert. Writing is the moment of the desert as the moment of separation."[36] Poets, like the Pharisees, must become "separated ones." "We must be separated from life and communities, and must entrust ourselves to traces, must become men of vision because we have ceased hearing the voice from within the proximity of the garden."[37] To give oneself up to the absence of the desert is the calling of both the poet and the Jewish people.

> The poet—or the Jew—protects the desert which protects both his speech (which can speak only in

> the desert), and his writing (which can be traced only in the desert). That is to say, by inventing, alone, an unfindable and unspecified pathway to which no Cartesian *resolution* can impart rectilinearity and issuance. *"Where is the way? The way is always to be found. A white sheet of paper is full of ways."*[38]

The poetic opening of language requires not only an absence from community and its old, fixed patterns of word use; it also requires the absence of the writer. We remarked on this earlier, but were unsure how far in this direction Derrida would go. Could he go the whole way of the complete egolessness of Aurobindo's Eastern thought? What he says comes close. To write, says Derrida, is to draw back—not into one's tent in order to write, but to draw back from writing itself. The poet must be grounded far from his or her own language. Poetic language must be emancipated, let alone to find its own way. The poet must know how to leave speech and let it speak alone out of the silence of the desert. In this sense there is a cycle of language for Derrida. Old speech, which has become rutted and has run its course, must be left behind. Leaving behind not only community patterns but also the structures of his or her own ego, the poet "dies" to former linguistic experience and is thus opened to the inspiration of the absence, of the desert. Then the poet is transparent to the pure possibilities of language. The poet is there only in order to provide a passageway. As Derrida puts it, "For the work, the writer is at once everything and nothing."[39]

Aurobindo shared many of these same ideas of the birth and decay of language and of the originary role of poets, but conceived of the whole process in historical and evolutionary terms. His theory developed in the course of his efforts to interpret the poetry of the *Ṛgveda*. Taking his clue from Yaska's ancient Sanskrit lexicon, the *Nirukta*[40] and Sāyaṇa's later Commentary on the Vedas (based on Yaska), Aurobindo develops the idea of the "multisignificance of roots."[41] In many respects Aurobindo simply followed the lead of Dayānanda,[42] who freely used this old Indian philology to suggest that the words of the Veda had a double significance. On the one hand the poems of the Veda can be seen as a book of religious ritual, on the other as a book of divine knowledge.[43] The Brahmanas are a development of the ritual aspect of the original Vedic poem whereas the Upaniṣadic dialogues develop the mystical or divine knowledge aspect. This clue, with its emphasis on the double sense of poetic words, also provided the basis for Aurobindo's analysis of language.

Aurobindo maintained that the ancient mystics discovered the true knowledge and sacredness of life. This wisdom was, in their view, unfit for and perhaps even dangerous to the ordinary human mind. If revealed to the vulgar and unpurified person such knowledge was in danger of perversion and misuse: "Hence they favoured the existence of an outer worship, effective but imperfect for the profane, an inner discipline for the initiate, and clothed their language in words and images which had, equally, a spiritual sense for the elect, a concrete sense for the mass of ordinary worshippers."[44] Seen in this light the Vedic poems are composed in symbolic language that contains an outer ritual framework and an inner mystic meaning. For

Aurobindo this is not just the secret of the Vedas but the clue to the way that all language functions. Language, when seen fully, has an external and internal sense. Whereas the Rishis and the early Greek mystics understood and used this double sense of language, modern philology, says Aurobindo, has failed to discover it.[45]

Aurobindo's imaginative reconstruction of the Vedic Rishi's psychological experience of the word is instructive:

> In that original epoch thought proceeded by other methods than those of our logical reasoning and speech accepted modes of expression which in our modern habits would be inadmissible. The wisest then depended on inner experience and the suggestions of the intuitive mind for all knowledge that ranged beyond mankind's ordinary perceptions and daily activities. Their aim was illumination, not logical conviction, their ideal the inspired seer, not the accurate reasoner. . . . The Rishi was not the individual composer of the hymn, but the seer (*draṣṭā*) of an eternal truth and an impersonal knowledge. The language of the Veda itself is *śruti,* a rhythm not composed by the intellect but heard, a divine Word that came vibrating out of the Infinite to the inner audience of the man who had previously made himself fit for the impersonal knowledge.[46]

Knowledge through language, especially Vedic language, comes to one who has a purified consciousness. Such purification progresses gradually by self-effort. It is not miraculous or supernatural. It is open to all who make the effort to travel the path of Truth. "On that path, as it advances, it also ascends; new vistas of power and light open to its aspiration; it wins by a heroic effort its enlarged spiritual possession."[47] The *Ṛgveda* is seen by Aurobindo as a historical record of such an achievement by humanity. At the summit of his spiritual journey the Rishi, in omniscient vision, functions like the cosmic scribe, pictured by Aurobindo in his poem *Savitri:*

There in a hidden chamber closed and mute
Are kept the record graphs of the cosmic scribe,
And there the tables of the sacred Law,
There is the Book of Being's index page,
The text and the glossary of the Vedic truth
Are there; the rhythms and metres of the stars
Significant of the movements of our fate:
The symbol powers of number and form,
And the secret code of the history of the world
And Nature's correspondence with the soul
Are written in the mystic heart of life.
In the glow of the Spirit's room of memories
He could recover the luminous marginal notes
Dotting with light the crabbed ambiguous scroll,
Rescue the preamble and the saving clause
Of the dark Agreement by which all is ruled
That rises from material Nature's sleep
To clothe the Everlasting in new shapes.[48]

In the hymns of the *Ṛgveda,* says Aurobindo, we find the Rishis repeating the same notions in a fixed symbolic language. There is an apparent indifference to any search for poetic originality or freshness of language. "No pursuit of aesthetic grace, richness or beauty induces these mystic poets to vary the consecrated form which has become for them a sort of divine algebra transmitting the eternal formulae of the Knowledge to the continuous succession of the initiates."[49]

Aurobindo speculates that the fixed relation found in Vedic language between the different notions and the cherished terms would not be possible in the beginnings of thought. The *Ṛgveda* we possess may well represent not the start but the close of a period. It is perhaps the legacy of "the Age of Intuition" bequeathed to a human race already turning in spirit toward the Iron Age and the lower levels of physical life, intellect, and reason. Thus the subsequent focus of Sāyaṇa and the modern interpreters on the outer forms of language and the Veda and the consequent loss of sensitivity to the inner spirit. Dayānanda attempted to revive this spiritual sensitivity, and Aurobindo sees himself as taking the process a step further. The goal is the recovery of the double sense of language and with it a transforming experience of the inner intuitive knowledge of the Vedic hymns.

Aurobindo believed that the world, in both its Eastern and Western developments, is remaking itself under a great spiritual pressure. The strong poetic literatures of the past may prove unable to respond to the enlarged breadth of vision demanded and may fall into decadence. New poetical literatures, sensitive to the inner and the outer aspects of the word in all their contemporary complexities, may be born. Language, said Aurobindo, passes through cycles of birth, growth, and decay. It stagnates by overattachment to its past traditions, or, "exhausted in its creative vigour, it passes into that attractive but dangerous phase of art for art's sake which makes of poetry no longer a high and fine outpouring of the soul and the life, but a hedonistic indulgence and dilettantism of the intelligence."[50] In Aurobindo's judgement English poetry, and the other European literary tongues, are currently exhibiting such signs of aging. The challenge to contemporary poets is to break free from deadening encapsulations of the sort represented by "art for art's sake" and to rediscover the deeper springs of poetry. In this task we can learn from the Vedic Rishis and the Greek mystic poets to open ourselves to all the potentialities of the World of Nature and to hear again the divine vibrations of the Transcendent. By bringing these two aspects of the word together in new ways, future poetry will effect a larger cosmic vision:

> a realising of the godhead in the world and in man, of his divine possibilities as well as of the greatness of the power that manifests in what he is, a spiritualised uplifting of his thought and feeling and sense and action, a more developed psychic mind and heart, a truer and deeper insight into his nature and the meaning of the world, a calling of diviner potentialities and more spiritual values into the intention and structure of his life that is the call upon humanity, the prospect offered to it by the slowly unfolding and now more clearly seen disclosed Self of the universe.[51]

Poets who most completely see with this vision will be the creators of the poetry of the future. If they successfully speak this vision they, like the Rishis of old, will provide the seed sound from which a new literary language will spring.

Aurobindo and Derrida both give a high place to the poet. To be transparent to the transcendent so as to be a fresh source for the evolution of language, as Aurobindo puts it, or to be absent to community and to ego so as to be open to the possibilities of language, including the *ruach* of God, as Derrida has described it—this is the poet's challenge. But for this challenge to be successfully taken up so that language can be renewed requires that the poet be freed from the scientific and rationalistic encapsulation of most modern language. Derrida has aptly termed this process *deconstruction.*

THE NEED FOR DECONSTRUCTION

Although both Aurobindo and Derrida agree that contemporary language use is in need of renewal and that the poet has a special function in this regard, only Derrida is specific about the process of language renewal. Derrida refers to this as a need for "deconstruction." This need, he argues, is seen most clearly in the way philosophy has used language in the West from Plato right up to the present day. It was Plato who expelled the poets from his ideal republic on the assumption "that reason could somehow dispense with language and arrive at a pure, self-authenticating truth or method."[52] Derrida sets out to deconstruct this assumption by demonstrating that reason, as expressed in the texts of the philosophers including those of Plato, makes its case by employing the very kind of figurative and metaphoric language that it rejects in the poets. Derrida's deconstructive reading of philosophical texts is aimed at showing that philosophers have been able to impose their various systems of thought only by ignoring or suppressing the figurative effects of language.[53] His approach to philosophical texts, such as Plato's

Phaedrus, is to highlight the often hidden use of metaphor and other figurative devices. Derrida's aim is not to do away with philosophy or reduce it to a species of literary criticism but to demonstrate that philosophical writing has no privileged status—that it makes use of the same kinds of language devices as other forms of writing. Once realized this critical awareness frees philosophy from its restrictive entrapment in reason—as defined by Western logocentric metaphysics—and opens the door to a philosophy renewed and enlivened by the full range of language use, inspiration, and criticism that it has at its disposal. In the end it is simply a recognition by philosophy that its data and medium is that of written language; therefore, it cannot escape either the richness or the limitation implicit in all language—especially language's figurative and metaphorical strategies. Derrida's goal is to show that philosophy, in its use of language, is no different than other disciplines; hence his deconstructive readings of literary, linguistic, and anthropological texts along side those of philosophy. Like the Indian philosopher, Nāgārjuna, Derrida's aim is to show that all use of language is limited by the human tendency to absolutize, to impose a metaphysics of presence,[54] and that this tendency has significant ethical implications. But more of that in the next chapter on Derrida and Buddhism. In the present context, the focus is on the essential poetic nature of language and the importance of this awareness for the realization of both the creative freedom and the limitations of language.

Aurobindo shares Derrida's view that language in the West has lost a large part of its vitality by an excessive concentration on science and rational philosophy. This has led to a false and stutifying view of language as objective and scientific in nature. In Aurobindo's theory of the double sense of language, the West has had an overdevelopment of the outer empirical word at the expense of the inner spiritual word. Although Aurobindo offers no specific corrective like Derrida's deconstructive strategy, he does offer a vague hope that the modern interraction of the occidental and oriental mentalities will have a helpful result. While the West has become overly focused on the outer form of the word, the East has engaged language more consistently at the inner level of spirit and soul. Both aspects are required, and the special role of the poet is to bring the two together—to be like the Vedic Rishi of old and fashion words that cross over from the spiritual to the concrete. Just as the Rishi's words provided a means by which the hearer and the chanter would be "tuned-in" to the transcendent, so also the poets words are to enlarge the hearer's psychological experience of language from encapsulation in the concrete word to an awareness of the word's inner spiritual soul. Aurobindo seems to assign Derrida's deconstructive task directly to the poets. It was Aurobindo's judgement that in the past Eastern languages and poets had carried out this task more effectively, thus providing a foretaste of the full realization for which we are still waiting.[55] But now the interraction of both East and West must be the parent of the poetry of the future.

> The whole of life and of the world and Nature seen, fathomed, accepted, but seen in the light of man's deepest spirit, fathomed by the fathoming of the self of man and the large self of the universe,

> accepted in the sense of its inmost and not only its more outward truth, the discovery of the divine reality within it and of man's own divine possibilities,—this is the delivering vision for which our minds are seeking and it is this vision of which the future poetry must find the inspiring aesthetic form and the revealing language.[56]

The poets' task, both East and West, is to keep language alive by engaging the inner levels of the spirit and soul. But this does not diminish the outward material side of life. Like Derrida, Aurobindo protests any one-sided overbalancing. It is in the creative engagement of both its inner and outer aspects that language can be vigorous and creative—open to its full possibility. Not only would this lead to an aesthetically alive and materially productive life, but such a vigorous and full engagement of languages would lay the foundation for world peace. World peace, in Aurobindo's view, will not come from a uniform language that is logically simple and scientifically rigid. Here Aurobindo agrees with Derrida's rejection of the totalitarian tendencies of absolutistic metaphysical language. Rather, says Aurobindo, peace will come from a sense of spiritual oneness that will arise in the midst of the vigor and enriching diversity of the lived languages of many cultures, East and West.[57]

Such an idealized vision of the evolutionary goal of language is not shared by Derrida. In his thought there is no evolutionary progress, only the constant need to deconstruct the absolutizing tendency present in all language, either Eastern or Western. The need for constant deconstruction is confirmed by our observation that whenever we speak we never say enough but always say too much. Yet always we are egotistically tempted to totalize or absolutize what we have said. Thus all speaking and writing, including that of Aurobindo and Derrida needs constant critical analysis to demonstrate its inherent ambiguity. Only through such deconstructive analysis will language be purified of its constantly developing one-sidedness and freed to the fullness of the originary trace (Derrida) or the multisignificance of root sounds (Aurobindo).

CONCLUSION

Derrida and Aurobindo are both sensitive to the "original" vitality of language and the difficulties involved in keeping that vitality alive. Although their prescriptions are often different there is much that is at least functionally parallel in their analyses of how language functions and what is now needed.

Both Derrida and Aurobindo conceive of language as grounded in a state of pure possibility (arche-writing for Derrida and the multisignificance of root sounds for Aurobindo) out of which a variety and flexibility of signification can arise. Both struggle with Freud's problem of how language can leave relatively permanent memory traces and yet at the same time remain perpetually open to the reception of fresh modifications. Derrida locates the possibility of language in the pregnant absence of the arche-trace, and is acutely aware of the anguish involved in the choice between the various possibilities of manifestation—manifestations in writing and speaking that simultaneously say too much and not enough. By contrast Aurobindo takes a historical and evolutionary perspective locating the loss of possibility early in history at the origins of Aryan speech and in the speaking of the Vedas. Unlike the fixed forms of modern speech, the earlier forms of language were seen by Aurobindo to be fluid and multisignificant. Language evolved from the general to the particular with a double sense of meaning, an inner or spiritual sense and an outer or empirical meaning. Aurobindo used this theory to provide new translations of classical Hindu texts such as the *Ṛgveda*. Derrida also sees a double sense in the possible use of words, for example in the Greek *pharmakon,* which can mean poison or cure. He uses this double sense to give a new reading to texts such as Plato's *Phaedrus* and to suggest that writing can be shown to have a high valuation, contrary to the traditional interpretation. Both Derrida and Aurobindo agree that language must be kept free from fixed formulations or one-sided interpretations if its originary possibility is to be safeguarded.

Poetry is seen by Aurobindo and Derrida as having a special function in maintaining the freedom of language. Derrida maintains that the access to free speech is through the revelatory power of poetry. According to Aurobindo through the sensitivity of the poets to the inner vibrations of the transcendent language is composed that crosses over from the spiritual to the concrete, as exemplified in the *mantras* of the Vedas. Both agree that for poetry to fulfill this crucial function two kinds of absence are required: (1) absence of the routine structured forms of daily language use; and (2) absence of the poet's ego. Only in these two absences can poetic inspiration occur and the free formulation of language take place. The examples of this process offered included the experience of the Vedic poets by Aurobindo and the experience of the prophet Jeremiah by Derrida. Although Aurobindo claims complete transparency and a permanent loss of ego for the Vedic poet, it remained unclear as to how far in this direction Derrida would go. But even for Derrida it is clear that the poet must be radically separated from his or her usual language pattern—the image of going into the desert was invoked—so that poetic language would be emancipated and left alone to speak out of silence.

For this challenge to be taken up so that language can be renewed requires that the poet be freed from what both writers describe as the scientific and rationalistic encapsulation of most modern language. In Derrida's terms this is the need for "deconstruction." Whereas Derrida is quite sure that what needs to be deconstructed is the logocentric way philosophy in the West has used language from Plato to the present day, Aurobindo is rather vague about what needs to be done. He suggests that in evolving from its poetic origins language has become excessively fixed in scientific and rationalistic forms, thus losing its freedom and vitality. Aside from some hopeful suggestions regarding the benefits to be gained from a mixing together of the Eastern (more spiritual) and Western (more concrete) languages, Aurobindo really has no prescription to offer. And as modern language use in India seems to be equally modern in the sense of being dominantly scientific and rationalistic in nature, the coming together of East and West is unlikely to produce significant change.

Perhaps this is where the more pragmatic and formulated program of deconstruction could be seen to serve the needs of Aurobindo as well as those of Derrida. As we shall see the basic principles of deconstruction are very similar to those found in another of India's traditional approaches to language, namely, the philosophy of Buddhism.

Chapter Six

Derrida and Nāgārjuna

When we turn to the Buddhist philosopher Nāgārjuna (second century C.E.) we find some pioneering efforts at relating his thought to that of Derrida already in place. This is different from the situation of the previous chapters where what was offered was a first attempt at comparing Bhartṛhari, Śaṅkara, and Aurobindo with Derrida.

Perhaps the earliest attempt at relating Derrida to Nāgārjuna is found in Part 3 of *Derrida on the Mend* by Robert Magliola.[1] Magliola argues "that Nāgārjuna's Middle Path, the Way of the Between, tracks the Derridean trace, and goes 'beyond Derrida' in that it frequents the 'unheard-of-thought,' and also, 'with one and the same stroke,' allows the reinstatement of the logocentric too."[2] In short Magliola proposes that in Nāgārjuna we find the solution for which Derrida is searching.[3] Magliola's analysis attempts to show that Derrida's cursory characterization of Eastern thought as nothing more than variations of logocentrism—variations of identity theory—cannot stand up when Nāgārjuna's withering attack on all identity theory is taken seriously. In fact Magliola finds that in his destruction of the principle of identity by reductio ad absurdum analysis Nāgārjuna employs the same logical strategy and often the very same arguments as are later used by Derrida.[4] On this point Magliola seems to be correct. Nāgārjuna's *śūnyatā* (devoidness of being or self-existence) is as he says equivalent with Derrida's *différance,* "and is the absolute negation which absolutely deconstitutes but which constitutes directional trace."[5] Although this may prove to be an acceptable reading of the resonance between Derrida and Nāgārjuna, we will want to specifically question the degree to which this "constituting of directional trace" may take place in language for Nāgārjuna. We are initially doubtful about Magliola's statement that "for Nāgārjuna the 'beyond knowing' allows for logocentric, i.e. language-bound knowing (in a way which frees him from Derrida's quandary concerning entrapment in language); and still Nāgārjuna's 'beyond knowing' is not itself logocentric."[6] This statement does not seem to square with Nāgārjuna's and his commentator Candrakīrti's conception of language as *vikalpa* (imaginary or conventional mental conceptualization) with no grip on reality.

A more recent comparison is offered by David Loy in his article "The Clôture of Deconstruction: A Mahāyāna Critique of Derrida,"[7] now included in his book *Nonduality: A Study in Comparative Philosophy* recently published by Yale University Press. Like Magliola, Loy finds that Derrida's critique of Western philosophy fails only because it does not go far enough and that the needed *clôture* is found in Nāgārjuna. Whereas Derrida remains in a halfway house of proliferating "pure textuality," deconstruction à la Nāgārjuna leads to a transformed mode of experiencing the world.[8] Loy points out how Nāgārjuna is more systematic in his critique of all metaphysical views than Derrida. Whereas Nāgārjuna fully deconstructs both identity and difference as opposing metaphysical dualities, Derrida deconstructs only identity and remains attached to difference. As a result says Loy, "Derrida's single-deconstruction leads to the 'temporary' reversal . . . and/or to a discontinuous, irruptive 'liberation' from reference grounded in the search for unattainable origins, into the dissemination of a free-floating meaning beyond any conceptual *clôture*. For Nāgārjuna, this would only be the illusion of liberation, while remaining trapped in a textual 'bad infinity' which tends to become increasingly playful."[9] Because Derrida's deconstruction ends with "difference," it necessarily initiates a new swing of the pendulum of dualistic conceptualization requiring yet another effort of deconstruction. This seemingly endless proliferation, or dissemination (to use Derrida's term), is nihilistic, says Loy, if it has no other purpose but to engage in "linguistic free play." Loy does allow, however, that such a nihilistic end might be given a more positive Nietzschean interpretation in that for Nietzsche nihilism opens the way to a necessary revaluation of all values.[10] By contrast, Nāgārjuna's complete deconstruction of both poles of the conceptual dualities that compose language leads to a mode of experience not governed by them—to a real release.

What Loy's analysis makes clear is that, although both Derrida and Nāgārjuna employ similar strategies of deconstruction, Derrida stops short of the logical completion of his program to safeguard his attachment to "difference." Nāgārjuna, however, suffers no such failure of nerve and pushes his critique home, completely deconstructing both identity *and* difference. The result, from Loy's perspective, is that Derrida remains stuck in language with its ineluctable duality whereas Nāgārjuna realizes an experience beyond language and its dualistic entrapments. Loy's analysis pinpoints the differences between Derrida and Nāgārjuna most effectively.

In this chapter we will undertake a reexamination of Derrida's apparent entrapment within language to see if it remains as negative a result as Loy proposes. Also we will attempt a clear understanding of what is meant by the claim that Nāgārjuna realizes an experience "beyond language." Because Nāgārjuna does use language—witness his famous work *The Mūlamadhyamakakārikā*[11]—and his tradition, Buddhism, seems to value scripture—at least in the form of the teachings of the Buddha—we will examine the thought of Derrida and Nāgārjuna in relation to the Buddhist approach to language and scripture. The chapter will be organized in three sections: oral and written language in buddhist scripture, the limits of language for Nāgārjuna and Derrida; and language and spiritual realization for Nāgārjuna and Derrida.

Oral and Written Language in Buddhist Scripture

When we analyze the place of spoken and written scripture in Indian philosophy and religion, it is evident that the *āstika* or orthodox schools (with the exception of the Grammarian school) largely share the same logocentric biases toward Being and Speech and against writing as those described by Derrida as typical of Western metaphysics. For example the Sāṁkhya-Yoga, Vedānta, and Nyāya schools are structured in terms of polarities such as identity versus difference, soul or self versus matter, and speech versus writing. The second term of the pair is always of a lower status. Pāṇini's *Astādhyāyī* or Grammar is based on the sound of spoken Sanskrit[12] and clearly values speech over writing. As we have seen in Chapter 3, the Veda is seen as the criterion form of spoken Sanskrit.

Buddhism, it seems, may escape this critique. To begin with it has no revealed scripture that manifests a divine *logos*.[13] In taking the middle path between the opposites, it would claim to steer clear of giving either speech or writing a privileged position. But is this theoretical claim evident in practice?

In spite of its rejection of the notion of "revealed scripture" Buddhist life is lived from within Buddhist texts.[14] Indeed, of all the religions, Buddhism has the largest scripture in many different languages—Pali, Sanskrit, Chinese, and Tibetan. But for Buddhists scriptural words do not have a special status like the *vāk* of Hinduism. For Buddhists, words, even most scriptural words, are not divine but merely conventional—created by humans to solve practical problems in everyday life. Whereas words are necessary for the conduct of our day-to-day affairs, words function by imposing distinction or categories where ultimately none exists. From the Buddhist perspective the worth of scriptural words is instrumental not intrinsic. Only if they help us to get from ordinary life (*saṁsāra*) to enlightenment (*Nirvāṇa*) are scriptural words seen to have value. Although the followers of the Buddha held his words to have special power, "the idea that the teaching arose from insights achieved in a special state of yogic development, a state open and available to all who have the ability and the desire to exert the tremendous effort needed to achieve it, meant that the words based on the experience need not be considered as unique or limited to one person in one time."[15] Buddha operated in an oral culture. His words were spoken in a preaching or teaching context, and apparently none of them were written down during his lifetime. Tradition records that within the year that Buddha died (perhaps 483 B.C.E.), 500 monks gathered together at Rajagṛha (the capital of the Magadha Kingdom) to agree on Buddha's teachings and to codify the Rule of the Monastic Order.[16] Ananda is reported to have recited all the "remembered words," which were then approved by the whole community (*Saṇgha*). These words were passed down orally for several centuries until they were finally compiled and codified into treatises called *sūtras* (Buddha's teaching). Along with these *sūtras* the rules of conduct for the monastic community (*vinaya*) were recorded and included in the canon as they were also considered to be the words of the Buddha. The various Buddhist schools expanded on the meaning of the Buddha's words through philosophical commentaries that were also included in the canon as *ābhidharma*. Unlike the Sanskrit texts of the Vedas, the Buddhist scriptures have not been carefully preserved orally. Buddha's attitude seems to have been very open and flexible, everyone was allowed to recite the scriptures in his or her own dialect —which did not make for a standardized oral or written form. Thus the Buddhist canon has been passed on in three language collections: Pali, Chinese, and Tibetan (with many texts also in Sanskrit).[17] The Buddhist scriptures, today, continue to function in both oral and written forms. In traditions such as the Tibetan and the Japanese Jodo Shinshu the oral chanting of *mantras* occupies a central place, and throughout the world the critical study of written texts continues. For the Buddhist use of either the oral or written scripture, it is the dynamic unfolding of Buddhist understanding and insight that is important.[18]

With its open attitude to scripture in both oral and written forms, Buddhism would seem largely to meet Derrida's critical requirements. There is no privileging of the oral over the written, such as characterizes Western metaphysics or the Hindu Sanskrit Veda. The Buddhist emphasis on the instrumental function of Scripture as having value only when it results in a new realization that is lived in one's life also squares with Derrida's emphasis on the text as having no referent outside of itself.[19] For Derrida, as for Buddhism, scripture, whether written or oral, has only one aim: to make the reader or hearer self-aware, to induce a self-realization that is lived in one's daily life.[20] One must not become ontologically attached to either the spoken word or the prose text (which Derrida refers to as a corpse of language).[21] Such attachments must be exited from by the direct experience of self-realization.

THE LIMITS OF LANGUAGE FOR NĀGĀRJUNA AND DERRIDA

Loy's analysis, referred to earlier, has alerted us to the different assessments by Nāgārjuna and Derrida of the way language functions in self-realization. We will quarrel with Loy's view that Derrida's view necessarily ends in a nihilistic self-realization. But let us begin with Nāgārjuna for the interpretation of his perspective seems equally problematic.

Loy concludes that Nāgārjuna's deconstruction of the dualities of language "points finally to an experience beyond language—or, more precisely, to a different way of experiencing language and thought."[22] The first part of Loy's statement that Nāgārjuna's deconstruction of language "points to an experience beyond language" is suggestive of the interpretation of Nāgārjuna that has been offered by scholars such as T. Stcherbatsky,[23] T. R. V. Murti,[24] Mervyn Sprung,[25] and Gadjin M. Nagao,[26] and it is the line of approach that will be followed here. The second part of Loy's statement, "a different way of experiencing language and thought," indicates another line of Nāgārjuna interpretation that is especially evident in the Zen tradition. We will give more attention to this tradition in the next section of this chapter.

Nāgārjuna's thought developed as a direct reaction to the Ābhidharma Buddhist philosophers' confidence that we could conceptually know things just as they are. The Ābhidharma approach was to philosophically analyze phenomena for their specific essences (*svabhāva*). Such an analysis, they claimed, resulted in an absolutely true view of things, which they termed *ultimate truth* (*paramārthasatya*), in contrast to the relative, commonsense beliefs of the less insightful, which were termed *relative truth,* that is, worldly convention (*saṃvṛtisatya*).[27] The aim was to come to understand and accept the correct view (*samyaydṛsti*). Then, through meditation, one could actualize its meaning in one's daily life. Thus the Ābhidharma path aimed at a final awakening and cessation (*nirvāṇa*) through a graded, step-by-step process of understanding, meditation, and practice.[28] The sought after goal was a repetition of the experience of the Buddha Sakyamuni in the life of each Buddhist practitioner. The difficulty was that the Ābhidharma approach put conceptual knowledge at the center. Unless one had an ultimately true view of things (*paramārthasatya*), one could not hope to follow a meditation that would lead to liberation.

Nāgārjuna deconstructed the Ābhidharma view that one could arrive at absolute knowledge about reality and that this could be the foundation for an ascending meditation to release. In reaction to the Hindu *ātman* view the Ābhidharma Buddhists had made the mistake of swinging the pendulum to the opposite extreme and adopting a *dharma* view. Derrida would agree with Nāgārjuna's approach of deconstructing both extreme and opposing views.

Nāgārjuna's deconstruction (the basis of the Mādhyamika school of Buddhism) rests on the perceived discontinuity between the way the world is and what philosophy while engaged in metaphysical speculation thinks the world to be. Suspicious of any absolute claim made about the nature of reality (such as the Hindu and Ābhidharma claims) and equally suspicious of any epistemology or view of language allowing such claims, Nāgārjuna shows "that the philosopher engaged in such metaphysics is living a sick form of life, infecting others who take him seriously."[29] The only cure for this disease is to demonstrate the utter hollowness of all metaphysical claims by the deconstructive analysis offered by reductio ad absurdum argument. Nāgārjuna develops this approach in his *Mūlamadhyamakakārikā*.[30] Nāgārjuna's *catuṣkoṭi* or four-pronged negation shows the futility of attempting to take any sort of ultimate philosophical position. He demonstrates the utter emptiness of all ontological statements. "Subject/ predicate logic is useful for mundane purposes, but when it is used to make metaphysical claims it becomes a kind of deceptive referring act: saying "X exists" becomes the basis for the belief that X actually exits."[31] Psychologically, one has fallen into the trap of becoming ego-attached to one's philosophic world-view. This is not simply a case of falling in love with the theory we have created or adopted, it also plays the role of providing for us a shelter (*dṛṣti*) from the anxiety and insecurity faced by the ego when the partiality or ultimate emptiness of all world-views is realized. Nāgārjuna's aim is not nihilism and the psychological depression it might induce. Rather it is the freeing of one from seeing everyday reality through "philosophical glasses" that give only a partial and distorted perception. Nāgārjuna's *catuṣkoṭi* technique is a method for deconstructing the distorting philosophical glasses so that reality is no longer experienced through subject-object and subject-predicate filtering. Once this enlightened state is realized, the application of the *catuṣkoṭi* is no longer necessary—the philosophical disease has been overcome and the patient is cured.[32] The need, both psychological and epistemological, for metaphysics has been totally overcome. Reality is immediately experienced just as it is. But where does this leave language, especially the teachings of the Buddha?

Although both Nāgārjuna and Derrida agree that attachment to the language, even the language of scripture, must be overcome for the realization of truth (*dharma*), there is disagreement as to the degree to which language can participate in this process. For Buddhism, and Nāgārjuna in particular, language (including scripture) expresses merely imaginary constructions (*vikalpa*) that play over the surface of the real without giving us access to it.[33] Derrida, however, sees the dynamic difference that characterizes reality as also composing the nature of language itself. This enables language, through its inherent processes of difference to function as a means of realization. For Derrida language participates in the reality it manifests. According to the Buddhist critique of language offered by Nāgārjuna, such participation transcends the limits of language. This disagreement over the limits of language between Derrida and Nāgārjuna is all the more significant because both view the nature of the reality to be lived as characterized by difference (the Buddhist doctrine of *pratītya-samutpāda* implies that everything is in constant change). But whereas Derrida finds this difference (which is constantly changing, constantly deconstructing itself) to be the very essence of language, Buddhism places the locus of that difference outside of language. As it is put in Nāgārjuna's *Mūlamadhyamaka Kārikā,* the concepts, names, or designations of language are conventional; "they are not on the level of ultimate truth and cannot represent ultimate reality, which remains silent (*tūṣṇīṃbhāva*), beyond all grasping (*anupalabdhi, anabhilāpya*)."[34] This assessment of language as merely conventional is given further development by the Yogācāra School of Buddhism through the use of the technical term *vikalpa*. Vasubandhu, in his *Treatise on the Three Natures (Tri-Svabhava-Nirdeśa)*, defines *vikalpa* as a mental form or construction characterized by subject-object duality.[35] *Vikalpa* is the mind's ability to imagine the unreal forms of subjectivity and objectivity that are separate from and superimposed upon reality. Thus language, as imagined mental constructions, is limited to conventional truth and cannot represent ultimate reality. The result is a two level theory in which language is limited to the lower level of imagined forms of mental construction (*vikalpa*) that cannot touch the higher level of the real.[36]

This complete separation of language from the real would be attacked by Derrida as being just as unsatisfactory as the extreme logocentric position that identifies speech with the real. Derrida criticizes any view of language that privileges one opposite or extreme over the other. With regard to language Derrida could claim for himself the "middle path" that the Buddhists appear to have missed. By limiting language to the merely conventional realm and by ultimately negating speech into silence, Nāgārjuna is, in Derrida's view, one-sidedly privileging silence over speech and therefore is a suitable candidate for deconstruction. Derrida's critique of any philosophy that privileges one opposite or extreme over the other is indeed reminiscent of Nāgārjuna's own *catuṣkoṭi* or four-pronged negation of all extreme views.[37] Derrida would see the Buddhist doctrine of the emptiness (of reality) of language as being an extreme view. What it is missing is that language is not empty of reality but, to the contrary, embodies within itself the very dynamic of difference that is, for Derrida, the essence of reality. Whereas for Buddhism language is empty of reality,[38] for Derrida there is no experience of reality outside of language. Thus Derrida's often quoted phrase, *"Il n'y a pas de hors-texte"* ("There is nothing outside of the text").[39]

In agreement with Buddhism, Derrida establishes the movement of difference as fundamental. In the Buddhist doctrine of *pratītya-samutpāda* (dependent coarising) notions of difference and change are fundamental.[40] Everything in our ordinary experience changes all the time. In the Theravadin doctrine of *dharmas,* "a factual event (*dharma*) turns out to last for just one moment, and, as Th. Stcherbatsky put it, 'instantaneous being is the fundamental doctrine by which all the Buddhist system is established at one stroke'."[41] Every moment of experience is radically different from all other moments that are constantly arising in the stream of consciousness. Difference is fundamental. Derrida agrees. For Derrida even the most basic irreducible state that he calls arche-writing or trace is composed of the movement of difference and contains within itself the potentiality for all oral and written language. This intrinsic *différance,* says Derrida, permits the articulation of speech and writing and founds the metaphysical opposition between signifier and signified. *Différance* is therefore the formation of form and the being imprinted of the imprint.[42] It is all a dynamic movement that has no originary subsisting trace (such as the *logos* notion implies). The trace is simply the basic impulse for movement that composes consciousness and that as a part of its own movement, erases itself.[43] Here Derrida's thinking has much in common with the

Buddhist notion of our experience as a stream of consciousness that leaves behind no enduring trace of its passing. As Magliola correctly points out both Buddhism and Derrida take as their specific task the deconstruction of the principles of identity and eternality.[44]

But let us return to the main point of our analysis, the disagreement between Nāgārjuna and Derrida over the nature and limit of language. Simply put, the disagreement is this. For Derrida the inherent trace consciousness of language conditions all psychic experience from deep sleep to dreams to ordinary awareness and even to mystical states *and provides the inescapable mode for our experience of reality.* Nāgārjuna, by contrast, takes the inherent nature of language in its subject-object conceptualizing of all experience to be the major obstacle to the experience of the real.[45] Whereas for Derrida language is the means for the experience of the real, for Nāgārjuna language as *vikalpa* or imaginary construction is the obstacle (*avidyā*) to be removed, if the real is to be seen. To fully appreciate this difference, we must more closely examine Derrida's thinking.

Derrida uses *sign* to refer to the whole (like the *sphoṭa* of the Grammarians).[46] Although "sign" is "irreducible," it cannot be experienced as pure presence. Rooted within language, even in its most holistic form, is the pregnant push toward sequencing, spacing, punctuation—differentiation in time and space. But differentiated language can never manifest the whole of the sign. Therefore there is no full speech, no absolute truth.[47] This is the limit of language. Derrida here emphasizes the positive contribution of articulated speech. The sign as the linguistic whole is manifested in speaking and writing, and in the dynamic tension of that manifestation lies the real. For the Mādhyamika and Yogācāra Buddhists, however, language is much more limited than it is for Derrida. From Nāgārjuna's perspective the *vikalpa* nature of language means that it cannot participate in reality in any way. The subject-object predication of language operates on a level (*vyāvahārika*) that is totally separate from the level of the real (*paramārtha*). Language, although it may be functionally useful in day-to-day life, is devoid of any contact with truth or ultimate reality. Reality cannot be found in the tension between the dualities, as Derrida suggests. Reality can be experienced only when language is completely negated so that the *vyāvahārika* level disappears leaving *paramārtha* or ultimate reality fully revealed.[48] The real for Nāgārjuna is utterly devoid (*śūnya*) of the conceptual constructions of language. For Derrida, however, there is no second level. It is only a question of keeping the tension even between the opposites, through continual deconstruction so that neither extreme ever triumphs.

Language and Spiritual Realization

Both Nāgārjuna and Derrida agree that what is required is a deconstruction of the illusions of permanence, stasis, or presence that ordinary experience and many philosophies have superimposed on language. This is Derrida's prescription as to the means for the realization of the whole ("the sign"). The direct perception of the dynamic process of becoming of language (not as a process of static reflection or metaphysical opposition) would be, for Derrida, the realization of the whole.[49] We cannot name this whole "spiritual" for that is already to engage the vocabulary of metaphysical opposition. But to understand the whole as manifestation of the inherent *différance* of the trace is for Derrida the goal. To go from inscribed trace (writing) to spoken word and the arche-writing that prefigures and predisposes both, only to be thrown back again, in a continual deconstructive reverse, would seem to be Derrida's use of language as a means for spiritual realization. Although this may look like the Buddhist prescription of Nāgārjuna, it is not. The deconstructive reverse does not result in the silence (*śūnya*) of language, but rather in the realization that the dynamic tension in the becoming of language is itself the whole. For Derrida, all of this cannot be understood as mere abstract theorizing. The language we are deconstructing is our own thinking and speaking—our own consciousness. We ourselves are the text we are deconstructing, that is why, for Derrida, there is nothing outside of the texts. Deconstruction of language is the process of becoming self-aware, of self-realization.[50] For Derrida language is not empty (*śūnya*) but experienced, as itself an ontological process. As we speak and write, it speaks and writes us, impelling us to action.

By contrast Buddhism sees language with its imaginary construction (*vikalpa*) of the forms of subject and object as ontologically empty.[51] Rather than making us self-aware, these imaginary constructions act as obstacles to clear perception of the real. Thus the need for the negation of the structures of language for spiritual realization. Even the oral and written scriptures of Buddhism must eventually be transcended if *Nirvāṇa* is to be realized. Seen from an ultimate or *Paramārtha* perspective, all words, even those of the Buddha, are empty (*śūnya*) of reality.[52]

The contrast between Nāgārjuna and Derrida is clear. For Nāgārjuna language is empty of reality and must be transcended for reality to be realized. By contrast, Derrida sees language to be rooted in reality. Thus it is through language, continually deconstructed from its extremes, that reality is realized. Interestingly, for both Derrida and Nāgārjuna the realization of reality extricates one from entrapment in the extremes of language and frees one to act in accordance with the reality that has been realized.[53] For different reasons both Derrida and Mādhyamika Buddhism rigorously deconstruct all theology, philosophy, and ordinary language that objectifies our experience into false gods and unreal presences. For both it is the erroneous objectifying of language that obstructs our acting in conformity with reality.

As a footnote to the preceding comparison, it might be noted that, like the Mādhyamika Buddhists, Derrida too talks of "silence." In his essay "Cogito and the History of Madness," Derrida says that "silence plays the irreducible role of that that bears and haunts language, outside and *against* which alone language can emerge. . . . Like nonmeaning silence is the work's limit and profound resource."[54] This line of thought is given a spiritual resonance when in "Edmond Jabès and the Question of the Book" Derrida observes that the God of the Jews constantly questions out of silence—that meaning emerges not in propositions, but in the silences, the blanks.[55] But this silence seems somehow different from the Mādhyamika silence. Rather than being the result of the cessation of language, Derrida's silence is the origin, the source of all speaking, and yet a source that locates itself in the quiet between the sounds of God's voice and the spaces between the letters of his writing. And it is here, not in Nietzsche's free play of words (as suggested by Loy earlier) that Derrida seems to locate spiritual freedom. Language both ours and God's originates not in His speaking but in His keeping still—it "starts with the stifling of his voice and the dissimilation of his face. This difference, this negativity in God is our freedom, the transcendence and the verb which can relocate the purity of their negative origin only in the possibility of the Question."[56] This theme reappears in Derrida's "Violence and Metaphysics: An Essay on the Thought of Emmanuel Levinas." There it assumes mythic context of killing the Greek father, the Platonic *logos,* of killing speech until there is a primordial solitude out of which our ethical relationship to the other arises.[57] Out of this arises the whole discussion of "altarity,"[58] which could be fruitfully related to Buddhist thought, but for now we will avoid that temptation. Our present focus is on Derrida's development of silence in relation to spiritual realization. The preceding passages are strongly suggestive of an apophatic strain in Derrida. Indeed in a very recent essay, "Comment ne pas parler: Dénégations," Derrida deals head on with negative theology as an interpretation of silence.[59] Even in the heart of silence or solitude the trace of the other is always found, if only as a memory, and it calls forth speech. Derrida puts it as follows: "Prior to every proposition and even before all discourse in general—whether a promise, prayer, praise, celebration. The most negative discourse, even beyond all nihilisms and negative dialectics, preserves a trace of the other. A trace of an event older than it or of a 'taking-place' to come, both of them: here there is neither an alternative nor a contradiction."[60] In theological terms, says Derrida, God's speaking and, as in Levinas, his silence is the primordial trace that creates and calls forth speech and silence from us. This infinite trace creates the very possibility for our finitude.[61] Therefore there is no origin or cause for trace or *différance.* But it comes forth out of silence—God's and ours—a silence that is both infinite and finite. Derrida goes on:

> Language has started without us, in us and before us. This is what theology calls God, and it is necessary, it will have been necessary to speak. . . . Having come from the past, language before language, a past that was never present and yet remains unforgettable—this "it is necessary" thus seems to beckon toward the event of an order or of a promise that does not belong to what one currently calls history, the discourse of history or the history of discourse. Order or promise, this injunction commits (me), in a rigorous asymmetrical manner, even before I have been able to say I, to sign such a provocation in order to reappropriate it for myself and restore the symmetry. That in no way mitigates my responsibility; on the contrary. There would be no responsibility without this prior coming (*prévenance*) of the trace, or if autonomy were first or absolute. Autonomy itself would not be possible, nor would respect for the law (sole "cause" of this respect) in the strictly Kantian meaning of those words. In order to elude this responsibility, to deny it and try to efface it through an absolute regression, it is still or

> already necessary for me to endorse or countersign it. When Jeremiah curses the day he was born, he must yet—or already—*affirm*. Or rather, he must confirm, in a movement that is no more positive than negative, according to the words of Dionysius, because it does not belong to position (thesis) or to deposition (privation, subtraction, negation).[62]

Taking this as an indication of Derrida's understanding of spiritual realization, it is certainly quite different from a Nietzschean notion of a nihilistic free-play of language. Language is there infinitely as trace or *différance* and in its questioning from the midst of silence leads us to confirm ourselves in ethical action, not through the debate of thesis and antithesis, but in relation to the other.

CONCLUSION

Derrida's spiritual result is in many ways very close to the goal of Nāgārjuna's *catuṣkoṭi*—not to reduce the holders of a viewpoint or *dṛṣti* to nihilism, but to sensitize them to the interdependent (*pratītya-samutpāda*) universe, of which they are merely a part, and to act in conformity to it. Whereas language plays an essential role in this process for Derrida, even in the final state of realization, the situation would seem to be quite different for Nāgārjuna. For him the subject-object separation that language necessarily seems to create prevents one from reaching the spiritual goal while under its sway. As long as one approaches reality through the viewpoints or *dṛṣtis* of language, *pratītya-samutpāda* and one's necessary place within it will never be seen. Thus the necessity to go beyond language into immediate experience in which no subject-object duality is present. Language for Derrida is able to participate in that spiritual goal to which it points, but does not seem to do so for Nāgārjuna.

I say "does not seem to do so" because a recent article by David Loy has suggested another possible interpretation of Nāgārjuna that brings him much closer to Derrida.[63] Loy points out that the interpretation of Nāgārjuna offered by scholars such as Murti and Nagao assumes that a distinction can be made between an "apparent world" (mediated by language) and a "real world" is "irremedially metaphysical and inconsistent with the fundamental Mādhyamika tenet that saṁsāra is nirvāṇa. There is nothing gained only something [language] to be removed."[64] *Śūnyatā,* says Loy referencing *MMK* XIII:7–8 and XXII:II, is intended by Nāgārjuna to be a soteriological therapy, not an ultimate truth or ontological category. "In other words, emptiness, the relativity of all things, is itself relative; the ultimate truth, like the conventional, is devoid of independent being."[65] The end of views such as "ultimate" and "conventional" leaves the world as it really is—a *śūnyatā* or nondual world in which there is no linguistic or philosophical meddling. In a separate communication Loy comments, "If there is no subject-object separation between language and object, between signifier and signified, then all phenomena, including words, are *tathata,* "thusness." This is why, as we see clearly in the Zen tradition, language too participates in the reality it manifests . . . [otherwise] how could so many Zen dialogues have led to a realization on the part of the student?"[66]

This makes clear Loy's different interpretation of

Nāgārjuna as ending in a spiritual realization that is in one sense beyond language but in which language still participates. We will leave it to Buddhist scholars to adjudicate between these two interpretations of Nāgārjuna. For our present purpose we will simply observe that if Loy's analysis is adopted, then both Derrida and Nāgārjuna envisage a spiritual realization in which language continues to function—and in which (as in Zen dialogues) language is instrumental in bringing about the result. The way certainly remains open for a close analysis as to how Derrida's spiritual realization finally differs from the realization of Nāgārjuna when seen from a Zen perspective.[67]

Chapter Seven

Conclusion

This study has provided an initial demonstration showing that the "writing" tradition of Western philosophy, to use Rorty's term, and Indian philosophy can come together in constructive and critical dialogue—"as two strong men standing face to face though they come from the ends of the earth" (to evoke again Kipling's poetic image). For our "demonstration" we have focused on the philosophy of language as conceived by Derrida in the West and in the Indian philosophers Bhartṛhari, Śaṅkara, Aurobindo, and Nāgārjuna. The comparative analysis undertaken has not only identified a large area of common ground between Eastern and Western approaches to language (along with some marked differences), it has also served to highlight distinctions between viewpoints within either Eastern or Western philosophy. For example, the clarification that Bhartṛhari can not be taken as presenting a *vivarta* view of language similar to that of Śaṅkara was demonstrated in Chapter 2, and the fact the Derrida's deconstructive analysis is more affirmative than nihilistic in nature as was shown in several places (especially in Chapter 6). The gain of this East-West dialogue on the philosophy of language is not just in the building of a bridgehead between the two traditions, important as that is in itself, but the benefit is also one of a deeper self-understanding achieved by examining one's own thinking in relation to the thought of the other. More simply put it is sometimes through others that we come to know ourselves. Indeed Derrida would maintain that it is only in our dynamic relation with the other that knowledge can arise. But what specific concluding comments can be made?

The dialogue between the positions of Derrida and Bhartṛhari on the origin of language carried out in Chapter 2 did establish a new forum from which Indian philosophy can constructively engage modern Western philosophy and vice versa. We saw that for both Derrida and Bhartṛhari language at its origin is beginninglessly infected with a pregnancy of difference. Just as Derrida finds that even the apparently undifferentiated inarticulate primitive cry has inherent within an impulse of difference that shapes itself into articulate expression, so also Bhartṛhari sees the beginningless and unitary *Śabdatattva* to contain a power to manifest itself as the Veda and as speech at all levels of actualization. For both this inherent impulse toward differentiation displays itself through a sequencing via the powers of time and space. Language at its origin, then, is seen to be not the mirroring of a passive *logos* or divine presence, a separate other, but rather the dynamic becoming of reality itself. This natural and inherent impulse of language to manifest itself is referred to as a *psychic imprint* or *trace* by Derrida and is seen to functionally parallel Bhartṛhari's notion that language as *Śabdatattva* has within itself a pregnant power for differentiation. The dialectic of the trace that Derrida calls *différance,* out of which the past, present, and future of language arise, is shown to nicely parallel the production of past, present, and future by the powers of time and space—powers of the *Śabdatattva* in Bhartṛhari's theory. For both, also, the dynamic dialectic and evolution of language is seen to be inherent in the "free becoming" of language itself, rather than a result of the action of a separated God "playing" in the world.

This comparative analysis helps to distinguish Bhartṛhari's view from the Buddhist perspective on language, which also rejects God as a separate other, but does not accept language as the ground within which the becoming of reality is taking place. Also revealed, however, is a definite difference between Bhartṛhari and Derrida. Derrida would reject Bhartṛhari's confidence that one can have a pure perception or *pratibhā* experience of the word in which the tension and dialectic of language is momentarily held in suspense. Such a mystical experience of language is not possible in Derrida's analysis. At this point the disagreement between Derrida and Bhartṛhari repeats the views of other Western scholars such as Kant and Jung that a pure perception of the real transcends the limitations of human experience and is therefore simply not possible. Eastern views like those offered by Bhartṛhari, Śaṅkara, Aurobindo, Nāgārjuna, and others are incorrect because they are imagining a human experience that does not exist. As Jung put it, Eastern intuition is simply overreaching itself.[1] At its base this disagreement between East and West is a disagreement as to the definition of human nature, its epistemological and psychological (ego) limitations. In the Eastern perspective, shared by both Hindus, Jainas and Buddhists, human nature is inherently perfectible—a position that the West, by and large, does not accept.[2] This fundamental difference between Derrida and Bhartṛhari points out the need for a thorough study of Western and Eastern views of human nature and their philosophical implications.

Derrida is probably most widely known for his placing of speech and writing in opposition, and then seeming to champion the latter over the former. In reality Derrida is wanting to challenge and deconstruct all the polarities of language, especially when one side is given a metaphysical preference over the other; for example, good over evil, presence over absence, identity over difference, male over female, and speaking over writing. We have seen in Chapter 3 that Derrida's critique finds ready targets in the logocentric championing of speech in both Western and Indian thought. In its technique Derrida's critique is very similar to the *catuṣkoṭi* of Buddhist philosopher Nāgārjuna. But its intended result of finding Self in the midst of language has much common with Bhartṛhari. Just as Bhartṛhari rejects other Indian schools that equate the experience of Self with something external to language and consciousness, so Derrida finds the Western notion of a separate unchanging *logos* to be nothing more than a repression of the experience of difference within the psyche. For Bhartṛhari, and it would seem for Derrida, the experience of Self is the unobstructed experience of *Śabdatattva* or arche-writing manifested in the temporal dynamic of language.

For both Derrida and Bhartṛhari it is the pure

possibility of difference that is manifested as language. For both, the linguistic whole (the sign or *sphoṭa*) has an inherent force toward differentiation that produces the double manifestation of inner meaning (signified, *artha*) and spoken sound (signifier, *dhvani*). Derrida and Bhartṛhari emphasize the positive contribution of articulated or manifested speech. The *sphoṭa* and the sign (Derrida's whole) are manifested; and in the dynamic tension of that manifestation lies truth. Both avoid the Buddhist skeptical view of language or Śaṅkara's view that language is instrumental and cannot participate in the reality to which it points. Instead both see truth to be contained in the very dynamics of language itself. This comparison serves to demonstrate that Derrida's statement that there is no referent outside the text is not as nihilistic as it at first sounds, and that Bhartṛhari's *sphoṭa* is not just a theoretical entity, as much Indian philosophy has assumed.

Both Derrida and Aurobindo conceive of language as grounded in a state of pure possibility. For Derrida this is the a priori state of arche-writing or difference, the condition out of which all language arises. For Aurobindo language is grounded in the root sounds that contain the possibility for a multiplicity of signification to evolve. Both struggle with Freud's problem of how language can leave relatively permanent memory traces and yet at the same time remain perpetually open to the reception of fresh modifications. When the historical evolution of multisignificant roots has been pursued to its logical conclusion then, says Auro-bindo, the power of the word is exhausted and language needs to evolve backward to recover the power of original sounds. Derrida also means something like this when he refers to the prose book as a corpse of language that must be exited from—the purpose of deconstruction. For both the aim is to get back to metaphoric, poetic language where the power of signification has not yet been used up. For this to happen two kinds of absence are required: the absence of routine structured forms of daily language use and the absence of the poet's ego. Only then can the free formulation of language occur. All of this is more clearly specified in Aurobindo. Sharing in the Eastern assumption of the perfectibility of human nature, Aurobindo claims a complete transparency and loss of ego for the Vedic poet, a condition toward which the modern poet must aspire. Derrida simply evokes the image of going into the desert, of becoming separated from one's usual language pattern, and of experiencing an emancipation and silence out of which poetic language could speak.

Whereas Aurobindo is vague about how the backward evolution of language is to take place, Derrida is very clear. What needs to be deconstructed are the routine ways in which the logocentric philosophy of the West has used language from Plato to the present day. Modern rationalistic and scientific language has become encapsulated in its own theoretical separation from the world of practical and ethical action. Only a thorough deconstruction will reunite the two sides. Although Bhartṛhari agrees with Derrida that language must engage both thought and action, he does not hold with the idea of either a radical deconstruction (Derrida) or a backward evolution (Aurobindo) of language. Bhartṛhari instead offers a kind of scientific prescription as to how to keep the structures of language pure by following the prescribed rules of grammar as developed by the Grammarian school of Indian philosophy. The Grammarian scholars did not invent these rules but found them to be inherently evidenced in the speaking of the Vedic revelation by the Rishis—the Veda being the criterion manifestation of the *Śabdatattva,* and the Rishis being perfected human beings who could function as transparent channels for the manifestation of the Vedic word. As long as the daily use of language remained true to the grammatical rules revealed in the Veda and made explicit in Bhar-tṛhari's *Vākyapadīya,* then that language would retain its power and meaning. Neither deconstruction nor the backward evolution of language is required. Rather purity of one's language use (with the Veda providing the criterion of purity) along with the absence of ego knots of ignorance in one's human nature is needed.

The other two Indian thinkers examined, Śaṅkara and Nāgārjuna, offer a somewhat different challenge to Derrida, namely, the goal of getting out of language altogether. They switch the focus of language use more explicitly to the spiritual goal to be achieved. Whereas Bhartṛhari and Aurobindo would agree with Derrida that the goal to realize is still within the range of language (although Bhartṛhari extends this range much further than we usually think of it, until it includes all thought and even the divine), Śaṅkara and Nāgārjuna, in different ways, locate the spiritual goal to be realized beyond language. For Śaṅkara language as a part of *māyā* is paradoxical. Ultimately it must be transcended and left behind for Brahman, the real, to be seen. So long as word cognitions are crossing consciousness, the ground of our minds (which is nothing but the pure consciousness of Brahman) will not be seen and recognized for what it is. Instead, the superimposition of the word forms of language will trick us into thinking that they are real and obscure the supporting Brahman consciousness that our word forms are simply delimiting by their superimposition. To clearly see Brahman the obscuring word forms of language must be removed. The paradoxical nature of language is that only through the insight induced by a particular portion of language, namely the Vedas and especially the *Mahāvākyas,* can the obscuration of language be removed and the underlying Brahman clearly seen. Thus, for Śaṅkara, language, especially the language of the Vedas, provides the necessary means for realization of the spiritual goal, yet language itself must be transcended for that goal to be realized. Vedic language is like the thorn that may be used to remove another thorn that is causing suffering (the rest of language), or it is like the medicine (a poison) used by a doctor to cure an infection that is causing us grief (one poison, the Veda, removes the other, the rest of language). Once insight is induced by the *Mahāvākyas,* the real, Brahman, is clearly seen and the limiting function of language as obscuring the real is removed forever.

Our juxtaposing of Śaṅkara and Derrida helps to highlight aspects of Derrida's thought that are often missed. In a certain sense Derrida is seen to agree with Śaṅkara that reality is fully seen only when language is negated. In his essays on Jabès and Levinas Derrida strongly suggests that God is not known directly through the Book but only when we keep still. When God keeps still (i.e., does not speak) and we keep still, in the awe induced by His silence, we experience Him most fully. Indeed if God were fully present there would be no room for us to exist. Thus, suggest Derrida, it is His silence, His absence, that creates an opening, a moment of freedom for something other than God, that enables us to exist. But the content of this opening, on our human side, is that of a God who astonishes and questions us demanding moral action from the midst of His silence.

Already the significant difference between Śaṅkara and Derrida becomes apparent. Unlike the perfect stillness of the Greek *logos* or Śaṅkara's Brahman, Derrida, following Jabès and the Jewish tradition, talks of a God who constantly questions out of silence. For Derrida the ultimate silence experience of the divine does not cancel out ordinary language, as it does for the language of Śaṅkara's *māyā;* rather, it throws us back into our experience of worldly language. Freed from entrapment in the privileging of one of the pairs of opposites we are infused with a divine demand for moral action. In Derrida's silence is a dynamism, a divine difference, that is not found in the Greek *logos* or the pure consciousness, pure being, and pure bliss of Śaṅkara's Brahman. It is a reality that starts with God's silent desire to speak. Out of that silence comes not only His speech and ours but also, because of the questioning inherent in the silence, our freedom to act. The responsibility accompanying this freedom is found in God's written and silent questioning of us. But to be heard His speaking and ours must be silenced. This is the paradox of language for Derrida, a paradox in some ways similar and in other ways quite different from Śaṅkara's paradox.

Like Śaṅkara and Derrida the Buddhist philosopher Nāgārjuna also sees spiritual realization to result from going beyond language. Unlike Śaṅkara, however, Nāgārjuna does not suggest that language plays a necessary role in reaching that final realization. Neither the Veda nor the words of the Buddha, contain any special instrumental means for inducing spiritual experience. Although both Nāgārjuna and Derrida agree that attachment to language, even the language of scripture, must be overcome for spiritual realization, they disagree over the degree to which language can participate in this process. Although not all Buddhists agree, many scholars interpret Nāgārjuna, and his commentator Chandrakīrti, as seeing language expressing *vikalpa* or imaginary constructions that play over the surface of the real without giving access to it. According to this interpretation of Nāgārjuna, language does not participate in or point to reality but only obscures it. For spiritual realization to occur overt and inner language use must be silenced through the practices of philosophical reductum ad absurdum argument and meditation.

Derrida, as we have shown, disagrees with this view and sees the dynamic difference that characterizes reality as composing the nature of language itself. Thus, for Derrida, language participates in the reality it manifests and is therefore able to function as a means of realization. This disagreement over the function of language is the more significant since both Derrida and Nāgārjuna view the nature of the real in terms of difference.[3] Whereas Śaṅkara undoubtedly settles (behind his silence) into identity, Nāgārjuna (behind his silence) remains in the Buddhist tradition and its perception of reality in terms of difference, change, or becoming. But whereas Derrida finds this difference that is constantly changing, constantly deconstructing itself, to be the very essence of language, Nāgārjuna, as interpreted by his Indian commentators, places the locus of that difference outside of language. In Nāgārjuna's view the names and concepts of language that we give to objects are merely conventional yet, due to our uncritical ordinary mental function, we take them to be real. Because of that words and concepts function to obscure reality from us. Nāgārjuna's *catuṣkoṭi,* plus the prescription of disciplined meditation, is designed to expose our ignorance in confusing words and concepts with what is ultimately real. Once that confusion is cleared and language is seen to be unable to express ultimate reality and no more than a convention that is useful in practical affairs, then reality is seen for what it is in itself. Reality is not another level of existence beyond the ordinary world (Śaṅkara's *mokṣa*), but is this world seen as it is in its interdependent state unobscured by the metaphysics of language. In Nāgārjuna's famous equation *saṁsāra* is *nirvāṇa.* Thus the "beyond language" of Nāgārjuna is quite different from the "beyond language" of Śaṅkara. But for both Śaṅkara and Nāgārjuna language, itself, is ultimately empty of reality. For Derrida however, there is no experience of reality outside of language, even though, sometimes, the interrogative silence or spaces of language speak most loudly.

The counterpoint between Derrida and Nāgārjuna has led to a different perception of the difference between the two than had been suggested in the previous readings of Magliola and Loy. Rather than needing logocentric completion (as Magliola suggests) or as ending, at best, in a Nietzschean nihilistic linguistic free play (Loy's reading), we have uncovered a quite different view of spiritual realization for Derrida. As we concluded in Chapter 6, for Derrida language exists infinitely as trace or *différance* and in its questioning from the midst of silence leads us to confirm ourselves in ethical action—not through the debate of thesis and antithesis, but in relation to the other. In its sensitivity to our interdependence with others, Derrida's spiritual realization seems functionally very close to the *Nirvāṇa* of Nāgārjuna even though the path he takes to get there is very different. Let us refer back one final time to his essay on Levinas. Derrida there states his aim as liberating language for the encounter occurring beyond the opposite totalities of categories like good-evil, male-female, and identity-difference. The attempt to think such opposites, concludes Derrida, is stifling. But there is a liberating encounter:

> Face to face with the other within a glance *and* a speech which both maintain distance and interrupt all totalities, this being-together as separation precedes or exceeds society, collectivity, community. Levinas calls it *religion*. It opens ethics. The ethical relation is a religious relation. Not *a* religion, but *the* religion, the religiosity of the religious. This transcendence beyond negativity is not accomplished by an intuition of a positive presence; it "only institutes language at the point where neither no nor yes is the first word" but an interrogation. Not a theoretical interrogation, however, but a total question . . . the only possible ethical imperative, the only incarnated nonviolence in that it is respect for the other.[4]

Notes

Introduction

1. See Harold Coward and K. Kunjunni Raja, *The Philosophy of the Grammarians* (Princeton, N.J.: Princeton University Press, 1990).

2. A number of important analyses of this point have been offered recently. See, for example, Brian Stock, *The Implications of Literacy* (Princeton, N.J.: Princeton University Press, 1983); Walter J. Ong, *Orality and Literacy: The Technologizing of the Word* (London: Methuen, 1982); Eric A. Havelock, *The Literate Revolution in Greece and Its Cultural Consequences* (Princeton, N.J.: Princeton University Press, 1982); William A. Graham, *Beyond the Written Word* (Cambridge: Cambridge University Press, 1987).

3. Jacques Ellul, *The Humiliation of the Word* (Grand Rapids, Mich.: William B. Eerdmans Publishing Company, 1985).

4. Jacques Derrida, *Of Grammatology,* trans. Gayatri Chakrovorty Spivak (Baltimore: Johns Hopkins University Press, 1976); and *Dissemination,* trans. Barbara Johnson (Chicago: University of Chicago Press, 1981).

5. See Harold Coward, *Sacred Word and Sacred Text: Scripture in World Religions* (Maryknoll, N.Y.: Orbis Books, 1988).

6. See, for example, John Searle's comments on Derrida that focus exclusively on "writing" in his review of a book on "Deconstruction" in *The New York Review of Books* (October 27, 1983), pp. 74–79.

7. K. Satchidananda Murty, *Philosophy in India* (New Delhi: Motilal Banarsidass, 1985), p. vii.

8. Ibid., p. 13.

9. To this day in Indian universities religion is not a separate department but part and parcel of the subjects to be covered in the philosophy departments.

10. Translation by K. Satchidananda Murty in *Philosophy in India, p. 13.*

11. For a technical philosophical description of *karma* (a much abused term in modern Western thought), see Yoga Sūtras II.12–14 and IV.7–9. The following is a summary of *karma* as found in these passages of the Yoga Sūtras of Patañjali. *Karma* is described by Patañjali as a memory trace recorded in the unconscious by any action or thought a person has done. The Westerner should especially note that for Yoga a thought is as real as an action—in fact, in the Yoga view, we think first and then act, and thought therefore is of primary psychological importance. The karmic memory trace (*saṁskāra*) remains in the unconscious as a predisposition toward doing the same action or thought again in the future. All that is required is that the appropriate set of circumstances present themselves and the karmic memory trace, like a seed that has been watered and given warmth, bursts forth as an impulsion toward the same kind of action or thought from which it originated. If

one, through the exercise of free choice, chooses to act on the impulse and repeat the same action or thought, then that karmic seed is allowed to flower, reinforcing the memory trace within the unconscious. Sufficient repetitions of the same action or thought produce a strengthening of the predisposition (*saṁskāra*) and the establishment of a "habit pattern" or *vāsanā*. Such a karmic habit pattern or *vāsanā* is the Yoga equivalent for the modern psychological notion of motivation. The unconscious, in Yoga terminology, is nothing more than the total of all stored-up karmic traces from the thoughts and actions done in this and previous lives. The actual passages are as follows:

Karma has its origin in afflictions	—	*kleśamūlaḥ karmāśayaḥ* (Sūtra II.12)
It ripens into life-states, life-experiences, and life-time, if the root exists	—	*sati mūle tadvipāko jātyāy-yurbhogāḥ* (Sūtra II.13)
Those [life-states, etc.], as the fruit, are pleasant or unpleasant, because they are produced from virtuous or nonvirtuous causes	—	*te hlādaparitāpaphalāḥ puṇyāpuṇyahetuvāt* (Sūtra II.14)
To those who understand, all [of those] is indeed pain, because change, anxiety, and habituation are painful and [the life-states, etc.] obstruct the operations of virtuous qualities.	—	*pariṇāmatapasaṁskāra-duḥkhair guṇavṛttivir-odhāc ca duḥkham eva sarvaṁ vivekinaḥ* (Sūtra II.15)

In *Yoga Sūtra,* karma is equal to *vāsanā*

A Yogin's karma is neither white nor black; for[all] others, it is threefold.	—	*karmāsuklāḳṛṣnaṁ yoginas trividham itareṣām* (Sutra IV.7)
From the [threefold karma] there come the impressions (vāsanā) of only those which	—	*tatas tadvipākānugunānām ekābhivyaktir vāsanānām* (Sūtra IV.8)

are capable of bringing about their fruition.

In *Yoga Sūtra, smṛti* is equal to *saṁskāra*

[The process of impression] continues uninterruptedly, even though there is a time lapse between births, places, and time, because memory and memory traces are of one substance. (Note: here, *saṁskāra* is better translated 'memory traces', because unlike Sūtra II.15, *saṁskāra* is equated to *smṛti*.)	—	*jātideśakālavyavahitānām apy ānantaryaṁ smṛti-saṁskārayor ekarūpatvāt* (Sūtra IV.9) *Commentary states: kutaś ca smṛtisaṁskārayor ekarūpatvāt/yathānubhavās tathā aṁskārāḥ te ca karmavāsanārūpāḥ/yathā ca vāsanās tathā smṛtir iti/jātideśakālavyavahitebhyaḥ saṁskārebhyaḥ smṛtiḥ smṛtiś ca punaḥ saṁskārā itv evam ete smṛtisaṁskārāḥ karmāśayavṛttilābhavaśāveśād abhivayajyante / . . . /vāsanāh saṁskārā āśayā ity arthaḥ/*

Therefore, according to this: *smṛti—saṁskāra—smṛti;* the continuation of which is supported by karma (*karmābhivyañjakaṁ*) and *vāsanā* functions as the support for *saṁskāra* (memory traces) which produce *smṛti* (memory).

(I acknowledge the assistance of my colleague Dr. L. S. Kawamura in interpreting these passages.)

12. T. R. V. Murti, "The Rise of the Philosophical Schools" in *Studies in Indian Thought,* ed. Harold Coward (Delhi: Motilal Banarsidass, 1983), p. 1.

13. See J. G. Arapura, "India's Philosophical Response to Religious Pluralism" in *Modern Indian Responses to Religious Pluralism* ed. Harold Coward (Albany: State University of New York Press, 1987), p. 171.

14. Ibid., p. 185.

15. K. C. Bhattacharyya, *Studies in Philosophy*

(Calcutta: Progressive Publishers, 1958), p. 115.

16. Ibid.

17. Ibid., pp. 207–217.

18. Ibid., p. 207.

19. Ibid., p. 210.

20. Ibid., p. 212.

21. Ibid., p. 214.

22. Ibid., pp. 214–215.

23. Ibid., p. 216.

24. Ibid., pp. 216–217.

25. T. R. V. Murti, *The Central Philosophy of Buddhism* (London: George Allen and Unwin, 1960).

26. T. R. V. Murti, "The Philosophy of Language in the Indian Context," *Studies in Indian Thought*, pp. 356–376.

27. Susan A. Handelman, *The Slayers of Moses: The Emergence of Rabbinic Interpretation in Modern Literary Theory* (Albany: State University of New York Press, 1982).

28. Ibid., pp. 22–23.

29. Ibid., p. 33.

30. Ibid., p. 39.

31. Ibid.

32. Christopher Norris, *Derrida* (Cambridge, Mass.: Harvard University Press, 1987).

CHAPTER ONE. PHILOSOPHY EAST AND WEST

1. Richard Rorty, "Philosophy as Kind of Writing," *New Literary History* 10 (1978): 141–160.

2. Christopher Norris, *Deconstruction: Theory and Practice* London: Methuen, 1982, p. 129. See also John Searle's review of a book on "Deconstruction" in *The New York Review* (October 27, 1983), pp. 74–79.

3. This has already been undertaken in a beginning way by Robert Magliola, *Derrida on the Mend.* West Lafayette, Ind.: Purdue University Press, 1984.

4. For a masterful presentation of this position, see *The Central Philosophy of Jainism (Anekānta-Vāda)* by Bimal Krishna Matilal. Ahmedabad: L. D. Institute of Indology, 1981.

5. Christopher Norris, *Derrida.* Cambridge: Harvard University Press, 1987, pp. 11–12.

6. Ibid., p. 12.

7. Ibid., p. 234.

8. A. J. Ayer, *Wittgenstein.* London: Weidenfeld and Nicolson, 1984, p. 159.

9. From "The Principle of Reason," p. 9, as quoted by Norris in *Derrida,* p. 236.

10. See especially Derrida's essays "Violence and Metaphysics: An Essay on the Thought of Emmanuel Levinas" and "Edmond Jabès and the Question of the Book" in *Writing and Difference,* trans. Alan Bass. Chicago: University of Chicago Press, 1978. See also "Of an Apocalyptic Tone Recently Adopted in Philosophy," *Semeia* 23 (1982): 63–97.

11. *Deconstruction in Context: Literature and Philosophy,* ed. Mark C. Taylor. Chicago: University of Chicago Press, 1986.

12. Ibid., p. 18.

13. Ibid., p. 26.

14. Ibid., p. 31. This compressed version of Blanchot is rather dense due to space limitations. For a more complete presentation, see Taylor, *Deconstruction in Context,* pp. 30–32.

15. Ibid., pp. 32–33.

16. P. T. Raju, *Structural Depths of Indian Thought.* Albany: State University of New York Press, 1985.

17. Karl H. Potter, *Presuppositions of India's Philosophies.* New Delhi: Prentice-Hall, 1965. Potter is also editing an *Encyclopedia of Indian Philosophies* being published by Princeton University Press with usually one volume to a school. These volumes are most helpful to the Western philosopher as not only is a comprehensive and authoritative introductory essay to the school provided but also included are annotated English summaries of the school's primary texts. Of the philosophers covered in this study the volumes on Śaṅkara (vol. 3) and Bhartṛhari (vol. 5) are now available, but a study of Nāgārjuna has yet to appear.

18. P. K. Chakravati, *The Linguistic Speculations of the Hindus,* Calcutta: The University of Calcutta, 1933, pp. i–ii. These early speculations included reflections on the origins of language, the relation of words with their meaning, the question of whether speech is eternal or created, and considerations as to the nature of speech in its original state.

19. *Ṛgveda* 5.10.2 and 10.114.8.

20. *Sāṅkhya Āraṇyaka,* 33.

21. *Taittirīya Brāhmaṇa,* 2.8.8.4–5.

22. *Kaṭha Brāhmaṇa,* 12.5.

23. T. R. V. Murti, "The Philosophy of Language in the Indian Context" in *Studies in Indian Thought,* ed. Harold Coward. New Delhi: Motilal Banarsidass, 1983, p. 361.

24. *Bṛihadāraṇyaka Upaniṣad* 4.1.2.

25. *Taittirīya Upaniṣad* 1.8.1.

26. *Chāndogya Upaniṣad* 2.23.3.

27. See *Ṛgveda* 2.3.22 and *Māṇḍūkya Upaniṣad* 10.2.

CHAPTER TWO. DERRIDA AND BHARTṚHARI'S VĀKYAPADĪYA ON THE ORIGIN OF LANGUAGE

1. T. R. V. Murti, "Some Thoughts on the Indian Philosophy of Language." Presidential Address to the 37th Session of the Indian Philosophical Congress held in Chandigarh in 1963, and reprinted in *Studies in Indian Thought: The Collected Papers of Professor T. R. V. Murti,* ed. Harold Coward. Delhi: Motilal Banarsidass, 1983, pp. 355–376.

2. See, for example, Heintz Werner and Bernard Kaplan, *Symbol Formation.* New York: John Wiley and Sons, 1963.

3. Fritz Staal, "Oriental Ideas on the Origin of Language," *Journal of the American Oriental Society* 99 (1979).

4. Murti, "Some Thoughts on the Indian Philosophy of Language," p. 364. Murti cites *Mīmāṁsā Sūtra* 1.1.5.

5. Ibid., p. 365.

6. Jacques Derrida, *Of Grammatology.* Baltimore:

Johns Hopkins University Press, 1976.

7. Christopher Norris, *Deconstruction: Theory and Practice*. New York: Methuen, 1982.

8. This appears mainly in *Of Grammatology* but with reflection back to several essays collected in *Writing and Difference*. Chicago: University of Chicago Press, 1978.

9. *Of Grammatology*, p. 17.

10. Ibid., pp. 11–12 and 17.

11. *The Collected Dialogues of Plato*, ed. Edith Hamilton and Huntington Carins. Princeton: Princeton University Press, 1961. "Phaedrus," p. 520.

12. Ibid., p. 521.

13. See Satyakam Varma, "Importance of the *Prātiśākhyas*," in *Studies in Indology*, pp. 32–52. Delhi: Bharatiya Prakashan, 1976.

14. *Of Grammatology*, p. 314.

15. Ibid.

16. *Nāgārjuna. Mūlamadhyamikakārikā*, trans. Kenneth K. Inada. Tokyo: Hokusedio Press, 1970.

17. Robert Magliola, *Derrida on the Mend*. West Lafayette, Ind.: Purdue University Press, 1984, pp. 87 ff.

18. Christopher Norris, *Deconstruction: Theory and Practice*. London: Methun, 1982, pp. 18–19. See also Christopher Norris. *Derrida*. Cambridge: Harvard University Press, 1987, pp. 105 ff. One is reminded of Hillis Miller's comment, "Language is always there and the lure of getting back before it is an impossible lure. That doesn't necessarily make it transcendent, only that we are stuck in it."

Criticism in Society, ed. Imre Salusinszky. New York: Methuen, 1987, p. 232.

19. *Writing and Difference,* p. 20.

20. T. R. V. Murti, *The Central Philosophy of Buddhism.* London: George Allen and Unwin, 1955, pp. 121 ff.

21. *Deconstruction: Theory and Practice,* p. 33.

22. *Of Grammatology,* pp. 195–198 and 247. Animals in Rousseau's view exhibit no speech or song. Although he allows that birds whistle, humans alone sing.

23. As quoted by Derrida, *Of Grammatology,* p. 196.

24. Ibid., pp. 198–199.

25. *Deconstruction: Theory and Practice,* p. 36.

26. *Of Grammatology,* p. 198.

27. *Deconstruction: Theory and Practice,* p. 37.

28. For a review of the views of these and other schools of Indian philosophy, see Harold Coward, *The Sphoṭa Theory of Language.* Delhi: Motilal Banarsidass, 1986, pp. 29 ff.

29. *Deconstruction: Theory and Practice,* p. 41.

30. *The Vākyapadīya of* Bhartṛhari *with the Vṛtti,* trans. K. A. Subramania Iyer (hereafter referred to as *Vāk.*). Poona: Deccan College, 1965, vol. 1, p. 142.

31. *Vāk.,* I:142, *Vṛtti:*

32. See Madeleine Biardeau, *Theorie de la connaissance et philosophie de la parole dans le brahmanisme classique.* Paris: Mouton, 1964, pp. 266 ff.

33. *Vāk.,* I:2 and 3.

34. *Writing and Difference,* p. xvi.

35. Ibid., pp. 16–20.

36. *Deconstruction: Theory and Practice,* p. 247; and Jacques Derrida, *Edmund Husserl's "Origin of Geometry": An Introduction,* trans. J. P. Leavey. Stony Brook, N.Y.: Nicholas Hays, 1978, pp. 16–17.

37. *Vāk.,* III:9:4.

38. *Of Grammatology,* p. 60. See also *Writing and Difference,* p. xvi.

39. Ibid., p. 65.

40. As quoted by Derrida in *Of Grammatology,* p. 66.

41. *Vāk.,* I:51.

42. *Of Grammatology,* p. 66.

43. Ibid.

44. Ibid., p. 67.

45. Derrida notes that the pure trace is *différance.* It does not depend on speech or writing but is the precondition for both. Although the trace as such does not exist, its possibility is anterior to all expressions. This intrinsic "trace" or *différance* dialectic permits the articulation of speech and writing and founds the metaphysical opposition between signifier and signified, etc. *Of Grammatology,* pp. 62–65.

46. Gaurinath Sastri, *The Philosophy of Word and Meaning.* Calcutta: Sanskrit College, 1959.

47. K. A. Subramanian Iyer, *Bhartṛhari.* Poona: Deccan College, 1969.

48. It should be noted that the one modern commentator on the *Vākyapadīya* who clearly rejects such Advaitic readings is Madeleine Biardeau. See her *Bhartṛhari: Vākyapadīya Brahmakāṇḍa avec la*

vṛtti de Harivṛsabha. Paris: Publications de I'Institute de Civilisation Indienne, 1964.

49. *Vāk.*, III:9:14.

50. See, for example, the lucid presentation of Vivarana Advaita by T. M. P. Mahadevan, *The Philosophy of Advaita*. Madras: Ganesh and Co., 1969, pp. 236–251.

51. See Śaṅkara's "Introduction" to his *Commentary on the Brahma Sūtras,* trans. George Thibaut. Sacred Books of the East, Vol. 34. Delhi: Motilal Banarsidass, 1968, p. 3 ff.

52. An English translation of Helārāja's *Tīkā* is available in Peri Sarveswara Sharma's translation of the *Kālasamuddeśa*. Delhi: Motilal Banarsidass, 1972.

53. *Vāk.*, I:142.

54. *Deconstruction: Theory and Practice,* p. 41.

55. *Of Grammatology,* p. 67.

56. Ibid., p. 66.

57. Ibid., p. 67.

58. *Kālasamuddeśa,* see Sharma's "Introduction," p. 19.

59. *Vāk.*, III:9:23.

60. *Vāk.*, III:9:24. This, says Helārāja is Bhartṛhari's meaning of the term *vivarta,* which appears in *Vāk.*, 1:1 & 3:3:81.

61. *Vāk.*, III:9:74.

62. *Vāk.*, III:9:37.

63. *Vāk.*, III:9:41.

64. *Vāk.*, III:9:45, *Tīkā.*

65. *Vāk.*, III:9:46.

66. *Of Grammatology,* p. 50.

67. *Vāk.,* III:9:52.

68. *Patañjali's Yoga Sūtras,* trans. Rama Prasada. New Delhi: Oriental Books Reprint Corporation, 1978, III:13.

69. *Kālasamuddeśa,* 52. p. 76.

70. *Vāk.,* III:9:53.

71. *Vāk.,* III:9:74.

Chapter 3. Derrida and Bhartṛhari on Speech and Writing

1. T. R. V. Murti, "The Philosophy of Language in the Indian Context" in *Studies in Indian Thought: The Collected Papers of Professor T. R. V. Murti,* ed. Harold Coward. Delhi: Motilal Banarsidass, 1983.

2. Ibid., p. 363.

3. Jacques Derrida, *Of Grammatology,* trans. Gayatri Chakravorty Spivak. Baltimore: Johns Hopkins University Press, 1976.

4. Ibid., pp. 52 and 14.

5. *The Vākyapadīya of* Bhartṛhari, trans. K. A. Subramania Iyer. Poona: Deccan College, 1965. hereafter *Vāk.* I have also read K. A. Subramania Iyer's edition of the Sanskrit text with Professor T. R. V. Murti. An English summary of the primary Sanskrit philosophical texts of the Grammarian tradition of India along with a major introduction essay has been edited by me and K. Kunjunni Raja, *Philosophy of the Grammarians.* Princeton: Princeton University Press, 1990.

6. See Harold Coward, *The Sphoṭa Theory of Lan-*

guage. Delhi: Motilal Banarsidass, 1986, pp. 7–9.

7. See Harold Coward. *Sacred Word and Sacred Text: Scripture in World Religions*. Maryknoll: Orbis Books, 1988, Chapters 4 and 5.

8. Herbert N. Schneidan, "The Word against the Word: Derrida on Textuality," *Semeia,* 23 (1982): 10.

9. Jacques Derrida, *Writing and Difference*. Chicago: University of Chicago Press, 1978, p. 20.

10. Jacques Derrida, "Freud and the Scene of Writing," *Writing and Difference,* Chapter 7, pp. 222 ff.

11. *Of Grammatology,* p. 51. Grammatology, for Derrida, is the science of writing before speech and in all speech.

12. Jacques Derrida, *Dissemination,* trans. Barbara Johnson. Chicago: University of Chicago Press, 1981, Translator's Introduction, p. x.

13. Ibid., p. ix.

14. Ibid.

15. "Freud and the Scene of Writing," *Writing and Difference,* pp. 221 ff.

16. Ibid., p. 197.

17. George Cardona, *Pāṇini: A Survey of Research*. Delhi: Motilal Banarsidass, 1976, p. 142.

18. *Of Grammatology,* p. 3. In this regard it should be noted that a recent article by Zhang Longxi shows that Derrida's adoption of the view of Leibniz, Hegel, and others that Chinese and other ideographic (rather than phonetic) languages are mute, and thus free of Western metaphysics, to be wrong. As Longxi puts it, "Chinese

poetry is essentially *not* a script to be deciphered but a song to be chanted, depending for its effect on a highly complicated tonal pattern." See his article "The *Tao* and the *Logos*," *Critical Inquiry*, 2, (1985): 390.

19. As quoted by F. Staal, "The Concept of Scripture in the Indian Tradition," in *Sikh Studies*, ed. M. Juergensmeyer and Gerald Barrier. Berkeley: Berkeley Religious Studies Series, 1979, pp. 122–23. See also J. A. B. van Buitenen, "Hindu Sacred Literature," *Encyclopedia Britannica*, vol. 8; and C. Mackenzie Brown, "*Purāṇa* as Scripture: From Sound to Image of the Holy Word in the Hindu Tradition," *History of Religions* 26, no. 1 (1986): 68–73.

20. Christopher Norris, *Deconstruction: Theory and Practice*. London: Methuen, 1982, p. 18.

21. *The Collected Dialogues of Plato*, ed. Edith Hamilton and Huntington Cairns. Princeton: Princeton University Press, 1969, p. 521.

22. Derrida, "Plato's Pharmacy" in *Dissemination*, p. 149.

23. Ibid., p. 152.

24. *Of Grammatology*, p. 57.

25. *The Collected Dialogues of Plato*, "Philebus," p. 1093.

26. "Plato's Pharmacy," *Dissemination*, p. 163.

27. *Of Grammatology*, p. 38.

28. Ibid., p. 52.

29. The preceding sentences summarize pp. 57–63.

30. *Vāk.*, I:1.

31. *Vāk.*, I:2.

32. *Vāk.*, I:120.

33. D. Carpenter, "Revelation and Experience in Bhartṛhari's *Vākyapadīya*," *Wiener Zeitschrift für die Kunde Sudasiens* 29 (1985): 190.

34. Ibid. See also *Vāk.*, III:3:81 and III:9:17 and 26.

35. *Vāk.*, I:120.

36. *Vāk.*, I:122, *Vṛtti*.

37. Iyer's note 2 on *Vāk.*, I:122, p. 110.

38. *Vāk.*, I:123.

39. *Vāk.*, I:123, *Vṛtti*.

40. *Vāk.*, I:128, *Vṛtti*.

41. *Vāk.*, I:130-131 and the *Vṛttis*.

42. See Iyer's note 1 on *Vāk.*, I:132, p. 119.

43. *Vāk.*, I:132.

44. *Vāk.*, I:135.

45. *Vāk.*, I:132.

46. *Of Grammatology*, p. 63.

47. *Vāk.*, I:81.

48. *Vāk.*, I:9.

49. *Vāk.*, I:5.

50. *Of Grammatology*, p. 69.

51. As explained by Zhang Longxi, "The *Tao* and the *Logos*," p. 391.

52. As quoted by Ernst Cassirer, *Language and Myth*, trans. Susanne K. Langer. New York: Dover, 1953, p. 7.

53. Aurobindo, *The Secret of the Veda*. Pondicherry: Sri Aurobindo Ashram, 1971, pp. 48 and 203–214.

54. "Edmond Jabès and the Question of the Book," *Writing and Difference,* pp. 75–76.

55. *Of Grammatology,* p. 272.

56. *Vāk.,* I:88.

57. *Vāk.,* I:14.

58. For a presentation of the whole Grammarian tradition, see Harold Coward and K. Kunjunni Raja, *The Philosophy of Grammarians.* Princeton: Princeton University Press, 1989.

59. "Revelation and Experience in Bhartṛhari's *Vākyapadīya,*" p. 194.

60. Ibid.

61. *Vāk.,* I:12–14.

62. "Edmond Jabès and the Question of the Book," p. 76.

63. T. M. P. Mahadevan, *The Philosophy of Advaita.* Madras: Ganesh & Co., 1969, Chapter 8.

64. *Of Grammatology,* pp 46 ff.

65. One thinks here of the notion of *līlā* or the unmotivated free play of the divine in Indian philosophy—the free phenomenalizing of the divine.

66. *Of Grammatology,* p. 47.

67. Ibid., p. 48.

68. Ibid., p. 36.

69. *Vāk.,* I:123. See also K. A. S. Iyer, *Bhartṛhari.* Poona: Deccan College, 1969, pp. 61 and 68.

70. *Vāk.,* I:5.

71. *Vāk.,* I: 14–16 and 131.

72. *Vāk.,* I:20.

73. Harold Coward, "The Yoga of the Word (*Śabdapūrvayoga*)," *Adyar Library Bulletin* 49 (1985): 1–13.

74. *Of Grammatology,* p. 51.

75. "Revelation and Experience in Bhartṛhari's *Vākyapadīya,*" p. 199.

76. *Vāk.,* I:51. "The energy (Kratu) called the word, existing within, as the yolk in the pea-hen's egg, has an action-like function and assumes the sequence of its parts."

77. *Vāk.,* III:3:81.

78. *Vāk.,* II:144.

79. *Vāk.,* II:437–438 and II:143–145. For a more detailed discussion, see Coward, *The Sphoṭa Theory of Language,* pp. 119–125.

80. *Vāk.,* II:143–146. Trans. K. Subramania Iyer. Delhi: Motilal Banarsidass, 1977, pp. 60–61.

81. *Vāk.,* II:146, *Vṛtti.*

82."Revelation and Experience in Bhartṛhari's *Vākyapadīya,*" p. 203.

83. *Vāk.,* III:2:14. Trans. K. Subramania Iyer. Poona: Deccan College, 1971, p. 72.

84. See Jacques Derrida, "Structure, Sign and Play," in *The Structuralist Controversy,* ed. R. Macksey and E. Donato. Baltimore: Johns Hopkins University Press, 1972, pp. 248, 249, 264, 265; *Dissemination,* pp. 293–294; *Of Grammatology,* pp. 71–73 etc.; Writing and Difference, pp. 64–78 and 79–153.

85. See the book of Amos in the Old Testament. Habermas also traces Derrida to Hebrew roots, see

Jurgen Habermas, *The Philosophical Discourse of Modernity,* trans. Frederick Lawrence. Cambridge, Mass.: MIT PRESS, 1987.

86. Jacques Derrida, "Of an Apocalyptic Tone Recently Adopted in Philosophy," *Semeia,* 23 (1982): 63–97.

87. Ibid., p. 87.

88. Ibid., p. 94.

89. *Of Grammatology,* p. 54.

90. "The Philosophy of Language in the Indian Context," p. 376.

CHAPTER 4. DERRIDA AND ŚAṄKARA

1. Hans-Georg Gadamer, *Philosophical Hermeneutics,* trans. David E. Linge. Berkeley: University of California Press, 1976, p. xxv.

2. Ibid.

3. Karl H. Potter, *Advaita Vedānta up to Śaṃkara and His Pupils.* Princeton: Princeton University Press, 1981, p. 14. This volume provides an excellent philosophical introduction to Śaṅkara as well as including annotated English summaries of the primary Advaita Vedānta philosophic texts.

4. Ibid., p. 46.

5. Jacques Derrida, "Edmond Jabès and the Question of the Book," in *Writing and Difference,* trans. Alan Bass. Chicago: University of Chicago Press, 1978, p. 67.

6. Śaṅkara never defines Brahman, but gives pointers or clues to Brahman's divine nature as being *sat* (pure being), *cit* (pure consciousness), and *ānanda*

(pure bliss). Brahman has no wants or desires.

7. "Edmond Jabès and the Question of the Book," p. 67.

8. *Advaita Vedānta up to Śaṃkara and His Pupils,* p. 52.

9. Śaṅkara, *Bṛhadāraṇyakabhāṣya* I.4.7, as summarized by Potter, ibid., p. 186.

10. "Edmond Jabès and the Question of the Book," p. 71.

11. *Bṛhadāraṇyakabhāṣya,* II.1.20, in *Advaita Vedānta up to Śaṃkara and His Pupils,* p. 191.

12. Ibid., p. 54.

13. *Of Grammatology,* p. 52.

14. Ibid., pp. 57–63.

15. Jacques Derrida, *Dissemination,* trans. Barbara Johnston. Chicago: University of Chicago Press, 1981. Translators Introduction, p. x.

16. *Of Grammatology,* p. 212.

17. Ibid., p. 244.

18. *Advaita Vedānta up to Śaṃkara and His Pupils,* p. 46.

19. Ibid., p. 52.

20. Śaṅkara is careful to point out, over against Maṇḍana, that meditation, from the passage in scripture that advises us to hear, think, and reflect (*śravaṇa, manana, nididhyāsana*), cannot be construed as an action (as Maṇḍana Miśra does) for liberation is not a *result,* and so cannot be reached by any activity, even meditation (see ibid., p. 52).

21. *Of Grammatology,* pp. 46 ff.

22. Ibid., p. 47.

23. See, for example, the book of the prophet Amos in the Old Testament.

24. Jacques Derrida, "Of an Apocalyptic Tone Recently Adopted in Philosophy," *Semeia* 23 (1982): 94.

25. *Writing and Difference,* pp. 79–153.

26. See Christopher Norris, *Derrida.* Cambridge: Harvard University Press, 1987, pp. 230–237.

27. *Writing and Difference,* p. 83.

28. Ibid.

29. Ibid., p. 90.

30. Martin Buber, *I and Thou,* trans. R. G. Smith. New York: Charles Scribner's Sons, 1958.

31. *Writing and Difference,* p. 108.

32. Ibid., p. 116.

33. Ibid., p. 151.

34. Ibid., p. 108.

35. Ibid.

36. Ibid., p. 109.

37. *Advaita Vedānta up to Śaṃkara and His Pupils,* p. 54.

38. *Of Grammatology,* p. 54.

CHAPTER 5. DERRIDA AND AUROBINDO

1. Jacques Derrida, "Freud and the Scene of Writing," *Writing and Difference,* Chicago: University of Chicago Press, 1978, p. 216.

2. Aurobindo Ghose, *Savitri* (Book 1, Canto V),

Birth Centenary Library (hereafter *BCL*). Pondicherry: Sri Aurobindo Ashram, 1971, vol. 29, 1969.

3. Aurobindo, "Diversity in Oneness," *BCL,* vol. 15, 1971, p. 492.

4. Ibid., p. 496.

5. *The Vākyapadīya of* Bhartṛhari, trans. K. A. Subramania Iyer. Poona: Deccan College, 1965 (hereafter *Vāk.*), I:81.

6. Jacques Derrida, *Of Grammatology,* trans. G. C. Spivak. Baltimore: Johns Hopkins University Press, 1976, p. 63.

7. Ibid., pp. 57–63.

8. Aurobindo Ghose, *The Secret of the Veda.* Pondicherry: Sri Aurobindo Ashram, 1971, pp. 49–53.

9. Jacques Derrida, in "Force and Signification," *Writing and Difference,* trans. Alan Bass. Chicago: University of Chicago Press, 1978, p. 9.

10. Ibid., p. 12.

11. *The Secret of the Veda,* Appendix II, pp. 551–581.

12. Ibid., pp. 563–564.

13. The following summary is based on ibid., pp. 49–53 and Appendix II.

14. Ibid., p. 49.

15. Ibid., p. 50.

16. See *BCL* vols. 4, 8, 10, 11, and 12.

17. *The Secret of the Veda,* p. 51.

18. Ibid.

19. Ibid.

20. Ibid., pp. 171–172. Here Aurobindo differs with Bhartṛhari who maintains that Brahman is *Śabdatattva,* both material and efficient cause of language and scripture. See *Vāk* I:1–5.

21. *The Secret of the Veda,* p. 52.

22. Ibid., p. 53.

23. Ibid.

24. The clearest description of Aurobindo's psychological theory of language function, as it undergirds his translation efforts, is found in Chapter 4 of *The Secret of the Veda.*

25. See "Plato's Pharmacy" in Jacques Derrida, *Dissemination.* Chicago: University of Chicago Press, 1981, pp. 63–171. In his reading Derrida is protesting the dominant approach of Western translators and commentators to take *pharmakon* in its references to writing to be consistently a poison rather than a cure. This, Derrida argues, has led to an unjustified downgrading of writing and a privileging of speech.

26. Christopher Norris, *Derrida.* Cambridge: Harvard University Press, 1987, pp. 37–38.

27. "Force and Signification" in *Writing and Difference,* p. 9.

28. Ibid., p. 26.

29. Ibid., p. 12.

30. *The Secret of the Veda,* p. 49. The term *mantra,* notes Aurobindo, signifies a "crossing over" through thought (root *man* "to think", and *tṛ* "to cross over") from the transcendent to the human levels. As *mantras* the Vedas are primary manifestations of the descent of the Spirit into the world, and,

through repeated chanting of them, an ascent from the physical to the spiritual can be accomplished.

31. *Writing and Difference,* p. 70.

32. Ibid., p. 8.

33. Ibid., p. 9.

34. Jeremiah 1:6.

35. *Writing and Difference,* p. 11.

36. Ibid., p. 68.

37. Ibid.

38. Ibid., p. 69.

39. Ibid., p. 70.

40. Aurobindo, *BCL,* vol. 30, 1969, p. 326.

41. *The Secret of the Veda,* p. 29.

42. Dayānanda, the founder of the Hindu reform movement the Ārya Samāj, took as his goal the reestablishment of the Veda as a living scripture. See Dayānanda Saraswati, *Satyarth Prakash* (2d ed.). New Delhi: Ārya Samāj Foundation, 1975. See also J. F. T. Jordens, *Dayānanda Sarasvatī: His Life and Ideas.* Delhi: Oxford University Press, 1978.

43. *The Secret of the Veda,* p. 29.

44. Ibid., p. 6.

45. Ibid., p. 28.

46. Ibid., p. 8.

47. Ibid.

48. Aurobindo, *Savitri* (Book 1, Canto V), *BCL,* vol. 29, 1969.

49. *The Secret of the Veda,* p. 9.

50. "The Future of Poetry," *BCL,* vol. 9, 1969, p. 286.

51. Ibid., p. 288.

52. Christopher Norris, *Deconstruction: Theory and Practice.* London: Methuen, 1982, p. 19.

53. Ibid., p. 18.

54. *Derrida,* p. 45.

55. "The Future of Poetry," p. 285.

56. Ibid.

57. Aurobindo, "Diversity in Oneness," BCL, vol. 15, 1969, p. 492.

CHAPTER 6. DERRIDA AND NĀGĀRJUNA

1. Robert Magliola, *Derrida on the Mend.* West Lafayette, Ind.: Purdue University Press, 1984, pp. 87–129.

2. Ibid., p. 87.

3. Ibid., p. 54.

4. Ibid., p. 88.

5. Ibid., p. 89.

6. Ibid., pp. 88–89.

7. David Loy, "The Clôture of Deconstruction: A Mahāyāna Critique of Derrida," *Indian Philosophical Quarterly* 27, no. 1 (March 1987: 59–80.

8. Ibid., p. 59.

9. Ibid., p. 60.

10. Ibid., p. 80, n. 43.

11. Nāgārjuna, *Mūlamadhyamakārikā,* trans. Kenneth K. Inada. Tokyo: Hokusedio Press, 1970 (hereafter *MMK*). The analysis offered will depend on

the exegesis of this work of Nāgārjuna's seventh century commentator Candrakīrti in his *Prasannapadā,* trans. Mervyn Sprung as *The Lucid Exposition of the Middle Way.* London: Routledge & Kegan Paul, 1979. Not having read these texts in the original, the analysis offered depends on working in translations with all the limitations that implies.

12. George Cardona, *Pāṇini: A Survey of Research.* Delhi: Motilal Banarsidass, 1976, p. 142. Sanskrit, as traditionally understood, is thus a prime candidate for what Derrida calls *phonocentricism* and is open to all the criticisms of logocentricism (see *Of Grammatology,* trans. Gayatri Chakravorty Spivak. Baltimore: Johns Hopkins University Press, 1976, p. 3).

13. See K. N. Jayatilleke, *Early Buddhist Theory of Knowledge.* Delhi: Motilal Banarsidass, Chapter 4.

14. Yun-Hua Jan, "Dimensions of Indian Buddhism," in *The Malalasekera Commemoration Volume,* ed. O. H. de A. Wyeseera. Colombo, Sri Lanka: 1976, p. 162.

15. Lewis Lancaster, "Buddhist Literature: Its Canons, Scribes and Editors" in *The Critical Study of Sacred Texts,* ed. Wendy Doniger O'Flaherty. Berkeley: Berkeley Religious Studies Series, 1979, p. 216.

16. *Entering the Path of Enlightenment by Santideva,* trans. Marion Matics. London: Macmillan, 1970, p. 16.

17. Edward Conze, *Buddhism: Its Essence and Development.* New York: Harper and Row, 1959, pp. 31–32.

18. "Buddhist Literature: Its Canons, Scribes, and Editors," p. 228.

19. Christopher Norris, *Deconstruction: Theory and Practice.* London: Methuen, 1982, p. 41.

20. Jacques Derrida, "Of an Apocalyptic Tone Recently Adopted in Philosophy," *Semeia,* 23 (1982): 63–97.

21. Jacques Derrida, "Edmond Jabès and the Question of the Book," in *Writing and Difference,* trans. Alan Bass, Chicago: University of Chicago Press, 1978, pp. 75–76.

22. "The Clôture of Deconstruction: A Mahāyāna Critique of Derrida," p. 60.

23. Theodore Stcherbatsky. *The Concept of Buddhist Nirvana.* Delhi: Motilal Banarsidass, 1968.

24. T. R. V. Murti, *The Central Philosophy of Buddhism.* London: Allen and Unwin, 1960.

25. Mervyn Sprung, *Lucid Exposition of the Middle Way.* London: Routledge & Kegan Paul, 1979.

26. Gadjin M. Nagao, "From Mādhyamika to Yogācāra: An Analysis of *MMK* XXIV.18 and MV 1.1–2," *Journal of the International Association of Buddhist Studies* 2 (1979): 32. See also Gadjin Nagao, *The Foundational Standpoint of Mādhyamika Philosophy,* trans. John Keenan. Albany: SUNY, 1990.

27. *L'Ābhidharmakośa de Vasubandu,* trans. Louis de la Vallée Poussin. Paris: Paul Geuthner, 1923–35, vol. 6, p. 139.

28. John P. Keenan, "The Experiential Content of Affirmation and Negation in Mahāyāna Buddhism." Unpublished paper, p. 4.

29. Jeffrey R. Timm, "Prolegomenon to Vallabha's Theology of Revelation," *Philosophy East and West,* 38, no. 2 (1988): 109.

30. This is nicely exemplified in the analysis of the statement "the human soul is eternal" offered

by Nāgārjuna and Candrakīrti. Candrakīrti asks what is the relationship between the subject, "the human soul," and the predication, "is eternal"; are the two terms identical or different? "If the two terms are identical, we are left with a tautology: the eternal human soul is eternal. If they are different and distinct, what could possible justify the claim that they are related" ("Prolegomenon to Vallabha's Theology of Revelation," p. 109). See "Self and the Way Things Really Are," in *Lucid Exposition of the Middle Way,* pp. 165–186.

31. Ibid., p. 109.

32. *Lucid Exposition of the Middle Way,* p. 151.

33. "From Mādhyamika to Yogācāra," p. 32.

34. Ibid., p. 32.

35. See Thomas A. Kochumuttom, *A Buddhist Doctrine of Experience.* Delhi: Motilal Banarsidass, 1982, p. 115. See also Robert Forman's definition of *vikalpa* as the mind creating a fictional world for itself, a mental construction or conceptual web on which individual entities or experiences can be placed (Robert Forman, "Paramārtha and Modern Constructivists or Mysticism," *Philosophy East and West,* 39, 4 [1989]: 401.

36. "From Mādhyamika to Yogācāra," p. 32.

37. *The Central Philosophy of Buddhism,* pp. 165–208.

38. Richard H. Robinson, *Early Mādhyamika in India and China.* Delhi: Motilal Banarsidass, 1978, p. 49. Robinson states the Buddhist position from the *Prasannapadā* as follows: "That an entity is empty means that own-being is absent from it. When the entities are pieces of language, it means they are symbols empty of object-content" (p. 49).

39. As quoted by Christopher Norris, *Deconstruction: Theory and Practice,* p. 41.

40. Edward Conze, *Buddhist Thought in India.* Ann Arbor: University of Michigan Press, 1970, p. 34.

41. As quoted by Conze, ibid., p. 34.

42. *Of Grammatology,* pp. 57–63.

43. Ibid., p. 61.

44. *Derrida on the Mend,* p. 88.

45. See Chandrakīrti's *Prasannapadā* as quoted by Richard Robinson, *Early Mādhyamika in India and China,* p. 49.

46. See Chapter 3.

47. *Of Grammatology,* p. 69.

48. *The Central Philosophy of Buddhism,* p. 86.

49. *Of Grammatology,* p. 36.

50. Ibid., pp. 49–51.

51. *Early Mādhyamika in India and China,* p. 49.

52. See the discussion of *Nirvāṇa* in Chandrakīrti's *Prassannapadā. Early Mādhyamika in India and China,* pp. 46–47.

53. Although Derrida keeps his spiritual self well hidden, his essay "Of an Apocalyptic Tone Recently Adopted in Philosophy" suggests that the apocalyptic (which contains a strong imperative for ethical action) be considered "a transcendental condition of all discourse, of all experience itself, of every mark or every trace?" (p. 87).

54. "Cogito and the History of Madness," *Writing and Difference,* p. 54.

55. "Edmond Jabès and the Question of the Book," *Writing and Difference,* p. 71.

56. Ibid., p. 67.

57. "Violence and Metaphysics," *Writing and Difference,* pp. 89 ff.

58. See Mark Taylor, *Altarity*. Chicago: University of Chicago Press, 1987.

59. The English version has just appeared as "How to Avoid Speaking: Denials," trans. Ken Frieden in *Languages of the Unsayable: The Play of Negativity in Literature and Literary Theory*. New York: Columbia University Press, 1989, pp. 3–70.

60. Ibid., p. 28.

61. Ibid., p. 29. See also Jacques Derrida, "The Infinite Differance Is Finite," *Speech and Phenomena and Other Essays,* trans. David Allison. Evanston Ill.: Northwestern University Press, 1973, p. 102.

62. Jacques Derrida, "How to Avoid Speaking," pp. 29–30.

63. David Loy, "How Not to Criticize Nāgārjuna: A response to L. Stafford Betty," *Philosophy East and West* 34, no. 4 (1984).

64. Ibid., p. 442.

65. Ibid., p. 443.

66. Private correspondence from David Loy, September 29, 1989.

67. David Loy is currently undertaking this task for a book titled *Derrida and Negative Theology* to be published by SUNY Press.

CHAPTER 7. CONCLUSION

1. See Harold Coward, *Jung and Eastern Thought*. Albany: SUNY Press, 1985, pp. 73–75.

2. See John Passmore, *The Perfectibility of Man*. New York: Charles Scribner's Sons, 1970.

3. As pointed out in Chapter 6, the Buddhist doctrine of *pratitya-samutpāda* implies that everything is in constant change.

4. Jacques Derrida, "Violence and Metaphysics: An Essay on the Thought of Emanuel Levinas" in *Writing and Difference*, trans. Alan Bass. Chicago: University of Chicago Press, 1978, pp. 95–96.

Index